WALLFLOWER

by gg renee hill

For:

My heartbeats

When I hear the word flow, I think of the faith of water. How it trusts its purpose and its journey so completely, with such power and obedience. How it changes form, shape and direction so gracefully. How it flows and sometimes it crashes, only to flow once again. Water is not afraid of its destiny as it surges, sometimes creating, sometimes destroying, too faithful to not be itself.

— *gg renee*

**Also by
GG Renee Hill**

The Beautiful Disruption

Writing the Layers

CONTENTS

INTRODUCTION

When you are quiet and reflective, someone who feels deeply and keeps the most unique layers of your personality hidden, it takes a courageous effort to listen to that small voice inside that nudges you to open up and let yourself be seen.

By denying this nudge, you are keeping a secret from the world that you were born to tell.

I hope you were drawn to this book because you want to feel empowered by your individuality and not impaired by it.

You want to slow down, reconnect with yourself and be more intentional about how you live your life.

You want to overcome the doubt and insecurity that has restricted your path in the past.

You want disprove all the lies you've ever believed about what you can and can't do.

You want to take up space and add beauty to the world.

You want to be strong through your setbacks, bold with your scars and confident with your choices.

You want to grow. You want to give.

I used to live in a world where I was not exposed to this kind of talk. No one spoke to me of self-love, softness and vulnerability as strength. Personal freedom was not an aspiration. I was taught to do what I was told and follow the plans laid out for me.

I expected that if I played along, the world would give me a reliable happiness. If I got the education, found the handsome husband, attached impressive titles to my name. If I was pretty enough, nice enough, and if I fit in with the right people, then maybe I would be successful and fulfilled.

But playing along was never satisfying and I didn't feel full like I thought I would. Every now and then I'd look in the mirror, into my eyes, and I'd see my soul looking back. A wave of recognition would pass through me, leaving a trail of hope, inviting me to follow it.

When I finally sat with my discomfort, and allowed myself to truly feel it, I opened myself up to the idea that if I could change my thinking my life could change.

I found purpose in getting rid of the things in my life that no longer served me and seeing what was left. I set out to discover how I wanted to live and what story I wanted my life to tell.

If you feel like your personality holds you back, my intention with this book is to inspire you to express yourself in your own way.

I see you.

You have silenced, masked and altered parts of yourself, but you are ready to be free.

You may be quiet, but you want to be heard.

You may be afraid, but you are not weak.

Through personal stories, creative inspiration and a writing guide at the end, Wallflower will help you peel back your layers to reveal your own stories, fears and desires.

With this awareness, you will be better positioned to channel your energy in meaningful ways and reveal the soulful, expressive woman who lives within you.

I

Quiet

I'M NOT CRAZY. I'M AN INTROVERT.

Being around people can be exhausting.

I feel much more comfortable interacting with people intimately, one on one. I'm friendly but quiet, often preoccupied with my thoughts. I've probably been perceived as standoffish from time to time.

It's not that I don't like people, but I have to observe my environment to see what part I want to play in it. I may choose to open up or I may choose to stay on the outskirts looking in.

At the risk of putting myself in a box, I'm going to say that I'm an introvert. That doesn't mean I'm not social or friendly. It does mean that I savor my time alone.

Psychiatrist Carl Jung introduced the concept of the introvert in his book *Psychological Types*. Jung's definition of an introvert is "wholly or predominantly concerned with and interested in one's own mental life," while the extrovert is "predominantly concerned with obtaining gratification from what is outside the self."

If ever a girl needed a self-definition, this was it for me. So many times I've doubted my sanity or thought something was wrong with me for being so socially awkward. I could be surrounded by people trying to outtalk each other and I'd be the quiet one wishing everyone would stop being so vocal and be more perceptive.

I struggle with giving access to people when it's not on my terms. I'd rather schedule a call than have someone call me unexpectedly. Confrontations put me at a disadvantage because I'm not able to take my time and process what's happening. I prefer writing to talking because it gives me the space and time to find the right words. When I talk too much I end up feeling like I'm depleting my life force.

These things will either sound overdramatic to you, or they will sound like the words of a woman after your own heart.

I used to think that I was shy, but now I know that's not the case. I'm just reflective. I instinctively take measures to preserve myself in social environments.

According to Susan Cain, author of *Quiet: The Power of Introverts in a World that Can't Stop Talking*, "Introverts are not necessarily shy. Shyness is the fear of social disapproval or humiliation, while introversion is a preference for environments that are not over-stimulating. Shyness is inherently painful; introversion is not."

I've been told that I appear confident and outgoing, and many people are shocked that I've ever been known as a shy person. But I've learned how to manage it so I can look confident and do what I need to do. When I have time to prepare for it, I'm quite social. But I need limits and buffers and escapes.

After a period of heavy socializing, I feel worn down, spent, drained of energy. Then I have to go be quiet for a long time.

When I don't take this time to recharge, I get cranky, impatient, and eventually sad and even depressed. I existed that way for years: constantly surrounded by people, constantly on the go, totally neglecting my need for solitude and wondering why I was so miserable.

And then one day I realized that much of my anxiety came from not knowing how to take care of myself, not only as an introvert, but as a soulful person who needs to find meaning in what I do to feel content.

Instead of fighting against my nature, I started thinking about how to nurture it. I stopped calling myself crazy. I stopped apologizing for needing time to be alone with my thoughts. With an enlightened view of myself, I learned how to set boundaries without feeling uncertain or selfish.

I've come to accept that I will always be torn between my inner and outer worlds. Slightly off the grid. Seeing things differently, experiencing things differently, stars in my eyes and fire in my bones.

I call myself a wallflower because I like to stay low-key, but I have a voice — I've worked hard to find it — and I want to use it. When I finally stopped resisting this truth, and gave myself the time alone that I needed, I began to see new possibilities for my life.

If you often feel overwhelmed and overstimulated, then please know you are not crazy or selfish or weird to value your solitude. It is important to protect your private time and put yourself first.

You don't need to apologize for being sensitive, feeling things deeply and longing for creative ways to express those feelings.

HIDING IN PLAIN SIGHT

I've tried to hide my heart for most of my life.

It always seemed to beat too loud and break too easily. I remember being a child in church trying to stay calm while the choir sang. With cotton candy hair and baby-oiled brown skin, I sat week after week, waiting for the music to move me. The holy ghost floated around the sanctuary on waves of harmonized sound, making people shout and jump up and down and raise their hands in the air. I was a quiet ball of intensity, moved by emotions I didn't yet understand.

I was timid, self-conscious, and afraid of embarrassing myself — especially around the black kids at church who said I talked white and needed more grease in my hair and the white kids at school who asked why my mom's skin was so black. I cannot remember a time when I didn't feel out of place.

I wanted to be perfect and fit in everywhere. Say-all-the-right-things perfect. Always-get-the-joke perfect. Cute-boys-like-me-and-cool-girls-want-to-be-my-friend perfect.

But I was shy. I knew that I wasn't the perfect, polished type, so I felt safest when I kept my true self hidden and tucked away. I was soft and that made me weak. I thought popularity and acceptance would give me confidence and criticism would kill me — death by sticks and stones — too sensitive to tolerate a harsh word.

By the time I got to high school, I was an observant people-watcher. I studied before I befriended, avoiding aggressive, confrontational people. I'd become more outgoing over time, fueled by the attention of my carefully selected friends — true friends that I still have to this day. We weren't the most popular or the least cool but we were safely in the middle and generally liked.

They made me feel safe to be myself. When I was with them, I felt unthreatened and comfortable enough to let my guard down, but I still had my secrets.

She wasn't diagnosed at the time, but my mother suffered from delusions and hallucinations, an undiagnosed mental illness. I didn't want anyone to know. By high school, it was impossible to hide. Within the circle of our family, we did not address her behavior. We did our best to live around it, like a door in the house that you don't open.

At a time when all I wanted was to be normal, I didn't know how to explain my mother's illness, so I did my best to hide it. I learned early on how to keep certain doors closed.

THE WALLS

Safely in the middle and generally liked.

Maybe this strategy got me through school, but I carried it into college and beyond as I continued to value fitting in more than standing out.

I was afraid to rock the boat, afraid to say how I felt if I thought someone would disagree. I avoided confrontation and debate. I was quiet. I liked being quiet. But I also felt limited by it because loud people seemed more powerful.

I didn't feel powerful — at all.

I excelled in school until I lost my academic scholarship after my freshman year of college. I thought I had a gift for dance until I auditioned to dance professionally and was cut during the first round. There was modeling and interning and promoting parties and selling jewelry. I kept trying new things and with each attempt, I gave up easily because all along I expected to fail.

I never knew exactly what I was searching for but I wanted to find something that would make me feel special and I couldn't articulate that, even to myself. I got good grades to feel special. I danced to feel special. I used men to feel special. I spent money to feel special. But no matter what I did, I could not escape the feeling that I wasn't special at all and my existence didn't matter.

How religiously I gathered my mistakes and misfortunes like bricks and built up walls of defeat within myself. Walls covered with goals I couldn't reach and dreams I wasn't strong enough to believe in.

Every criticism, every dismissal became a brick in the wall. Each failure, another brick. The walls grew with my fears of falling short.

Restriction camouflaged as refuge, I looked around at the walls and I blessed them. They kept me safe from trying and losing.

I firmly planted myself in the middle of the walls I'd built around me. I didn't want to say too much, work too hard or be too passionate about anything.

Time and again, we save our love, acceptance and optimism for other people and we direct all our doubts and negative thoughts toward ourselves.

As a result, patterns start to show up in our lives to get our attention.

II

Patterns

THE MOLD

When you want what everyone else wants, without discretion, you do what you see everyone else doing.

When you believe that what you see, what's presented to you, is all there is, you try to choose a mold to squeeze into.

Even if it hurts, even if you can't breathe, even if you have to cut off parts of yourself to make it fit.

IN MY OWN WAY

I felt like an imposter.

I was 17 with a shiny new internship working in the marketing department at a steel company. My mom made me wear these boxy pantsuits with shoulder pads that made me feel more awkward and out of place than I already did.

Soon after starting, I decided I wasn't smart enough to succeed there. I knew nothing about steel or marketing or how to add any value to this strange corporate world. My friends were working at the mall and I wished I was there with them.

They grouped all the interns together and gave us projects to work on throughout the summer. Everything was collaborative and daily we were put on the spot to come up with quick ideas as a team. They told us to think outside the box and bring our honest perspectives to each project.

Despite their encouragement, the environment brought every insecurity out of me and I was too intimidated to be myself and share my thoughts. When we were given an assignment and the pressure was on, my mind would not cooperate. I didn't believe that I deserved to be there so instead of absorbing the experience with my heart and mind open, I focused on keeping my mouth shut and staying under the radar.

The problem is this — you can't thoroughly experience anything if you are worried about embarrassing yourself. Your ego gets in the way of your natural flow and you play small, afraid of how people will respond if you are free and unashamed.

When I first got hired for the internship, I was thrilled. I was a broke college student, it paid fourteen dollars an hour and I expected it to be easy. Filing. Busy work. Training. Group lunches. Maybe a little market research. Maybe a presentation at the end of the summer. No problem.

On the first day when they told us to put together a presentation about the steel industry and the other interns seemed more knowledgeable than me, I was thrown. All it took was this first hint of a challenge, the fear of not being enough, and something inside me turned off. Deflated, I tried to hide my discomfort by being quiet and doing the bare minimum for the rest of the summer.

I didn't understand the growth that could come from showing up — especially when you're scared — and allowing yourself to be seen right where you are.

Five years later I tried out for a professional dance team. I'd just graduated from college where I danced for all four years. Prior to that, I'd had ten years of lessons. I was confident that I could leap my way onto any dance team or company that I wanted. I thought it would be easy.

After some initial screening, they separated us into two groups — technique and choreography.

The technique group would spend the day learning the proper way to do basic turns and leaps and some gymnastics. This group would not be trying out. Meanwhile, the choreography group would learn a routine and audition because the instructors saw that they already had the basics mastered.

I was placed in the technique group. The friends I came with all made it into the choreography group.

Embarrassed, I became consumed with feeling sorry for myself. I didn't leave the audition but I didn't stay either. Mentally, I checked out and I didn't absorb the free instruction or advice.

Hindsight shows me clearly in my own way, blocking two amazing opportunities.

Worried about failing publicly and facing rejection.

Wanting the rewards without the risks.

THE KNOT

There is a knot that gathers in your stomach when you're alone and afraid of facing yourself.

When you think that being rescued is the only way to escape.

I was convinced that being alone meant being unloved.

The thought of that made every insecurity I had feel alive and dangerous.

IGNORING YOUR HEARTBEAT

He figured me out too quickly. He got me laughing and feeling comfortable, making me want him before I knew him.

I knew that he loved my hair messy and my face with no makeup. I knew that he was young and unpredictable and I was drawn to him. His lips, his hands, even his crazy felt like home. He took me to meet his family. He learned the weird language I spoke with my friends and he spoke it fluently.

He was attentive then aloof then attentive then aloof. That was how he hypnotized me. I was convinced his attention could unravel the knot in my stomach and the withdrawal was worth the high.

I couldn't say no to him. I couldn't explain myself. All I could do was come when he called.

Being loyal to a lying man means ignoring your heartbeat, silencing your voice and diminishing your spirit. Pretending you don't want all of him so you can be content with what you get.

It means the thin line between love and hate keeps moving. You stop seeing clearly and the difference between real and fake gets blurry.

You find yourself trapped inside a repetitive story.

He didn't want to be with me, but he didn't want me to be with anyone else. He didn't love me, he idealized me. He saw what he wanted, his imagination ran wild and he made a character of me. He put me in a role I didn't ask for and I improvised to please him.

He went away but never stayed away. I said we were done but never meant it. We carried on like we had no choice. Break-up sex, make-up sex, I-love-you sex, I-hate-you sex.

I stuck around because I wanted the relationship more than I wanted the man.

So often our unrealistic beliefs about relationships set us up for disappointment and heartache, thinking that personal fulfillment should come as a result of our relationships instead of being a foundation upon which to build them.

He was supposed to rescue me, pick up the script I'd written for him and deliver passionate lines of devotion on cue. Never mind that he was a human being with needs, fears, strengths and weaknesses; not a faceless, dreamlike image that would go through the motions of loving me without any complexity or surprises.

I couldn't see him for who he was and he could not see me.

I was endlessly patient, thinking that if I was worth it, he would change for me. But he didn't change. So I decided I wasn't worth it.

Our love story was a reflection of my life.

Silencing myself to be accepted. Trying to bend and change myself. My neediness disfigured me and I couldn't see the shape of who I was meant to be.

When we chase the wrong things for the wrong reasons, we end up unfulfilled. We get so used to feeding lack to ourselves that we hunger for it, looking for ways to satisfy the craving and stay full with its emptiness.

When lack and loss are imprinted on your mind, you believe that you are never enough and you never have enough. That you are damaged, unlovable, and unworthy of more.

Living like this makes you weary.

The words you don't say.

The pain you smile through.

The time you waste.

EVERY WOMAN

She was nothing like me. I could tell by the things she said to him and the way he responded to her. She brought out a side of him I'd never seen before and while their exchange infuriated me, it also intrigued me:

Is this the real him? Does he keep these girls on the side to satisfy a part of him that I can't? Maybe he thinks I'm boring. Maybe I'm the quiet, good girl and he keeps his bad girls on the side.

I read his text messages everyday as a form of self-torture. I looked forward to the pain as if poking the wound would wake me up.

I thought, I'm not every woman to him. I'm not enough.

Pain sinks in slowly with me, vibrating in waves. I have delayed reactions like kids when they fall and the shock of it steals their breath for long seconds, mouth open, eyes wide, as the pain settles in and the cry builds up in their throats.

I was full of a ravenous self-doubt, hunting for proof that I couldn't win.

Obviously if I was dating a guy and he cheated, it was because I wasn't good enough to keep him.

Obviously if I didn't get the job I applied for, it was because I was just average, not smart enough or capable enough to stand out.

I wanted to be picked and I wanted to be praised to prove I was good enough.

I didn't believe I could keep my smile on my own, so I chased happiness, looking for someone to make me feel special and give me the attention I desired.

These misguided pursuits invariably ended in disappointment.

Love was not love, it was urgency and lack and pretending.

In *The Four Agreements*, Don Miguel Ruiz said, "Nothing others do is because of you. What others say and do is a projection of their own reality, their own dream. When you are immune to the options and actions of others, you won't be the victim of needless suffering."

I remember asking myself:

What can I do, how do I stop putting myself in situations where my happiness depends on someone else?

CONSEQUENCES

Every month we waited for the eviction notice.

Both of us employed, but somehow unable to manage our money and pay our bills on time. Every month we paid the rent by the skin of our teeth at the very last minute.

One time, we pushed it to the morning that the sheriff was due to come put us out. I remember sitting there in the living room looking around and imagining the booming knock on the door, the strangers in our home, the powerlessness.

Our treasures would soon be piled up and thrown out on the curb like trash. The picture frames outlining our smiling faces. The furniture we pitched in and saved up to buy.

It's in these dark moments, when we feel rock bottom and ashamed, that we judge ourselves most harshly. We look around at our circumstances and the most negative beliefs we have about ourselves seem to be proven true.

I made up my mind to surrender to what was happening. All I could do was breathe and sit with the situation I'd created.

This was just one of many storms going on in my life at the time.

Just like our creature comforts would soon be on the sidewalk, the consequences of my chaos were piling up all over my life. But I still wasn't ready to dig down to the root of it.

I sat there in the living room on that eviction day and made promises to myself and to God that I would ultimately break. I prayed and said I would change my ways and I'd be more responsible.

My roommate showed up with the money before the sheriff came and we were not evicted that day.

The next day, we invited friends over and spent some of next month's rent to celebrate.

SELF-DOUBT

I let it happen. Again.

I lost myself and decided not to trust myself. Again.

Because my instincts steer me wrong.

And I never learn. And I always end up back here.

Some part of me must want this. Because who am I without this?

Life begs the question.

Again and again.

AUDIENCE

I was a puzzle. He wanted to solve me and I wanted to see if he could.

A yearning for mystery connected us.

He was the perfect audience. He noticed everything about me, which made me aware and deliberate with my movements. In his presence, walking was foreplay more than function. Senses heightened, tilting my head to kiss him, I hung on his every word, never missing an opportunity to dazzle him with softness.

He watched me open up and shut down. I looked safe but I was slippery and he loved that. I wore my pain like lingerie under my clothes. Every glimpse made him want to comfort me, fix me; a devotion that neither of us understood.

There was something heavy about his love that kept me from expanding and his attention never felt quite right. I fell, I called out, he picked me up, I ran away.

He was sincere, but I needed my own attention, not his.

The smiles I gave myself, the salty sweet taste of my tears, the jokes that were only funny to me — these were gifts I overlooked and replaced with a longing to be seen. It was as if my world didn't matter if I wasn't constantly being affirmed by someone.

VICTIM STORY

He said I cry more than anyone he has ever known. He said when I'm low, I pull him down and when I'm high, he can't reach me.

He said I walk through life looking for every possible reason to feel wounded.

Some words float over your head. Some burn up before they reach you. Some crash into you and leave a mark.

His words created a clean slice that opened me, as if the pain wanted to confirm that he'd spoken the truth.

The victim was the most addictive role I'd ever learned to play.

I found depth in being troubled.

I was living a story about a girl, resigned to a life of brokenness.

She made herself a martyr and indulged in the role of being kind-hearted and unfortunate. A sad girl who smiles to spread happiness. An insecure and irresponsible, but open-hearted girl.

I knew that she wasn't all bad, but I convinced myself that her bad outweighed her good.

In my early twenties, I stopped doing two of the main things that made me feel like myself: I stopped writing and I stopped reading.

Instead of books, I studied men and relationships. I left behind the habits that were essential to maintaining my sense of self. No wonder I felt so lost.

As I wandered, toxic people looking for empathy gravitated toward me. This was my pattern: Allowing people to mistreat me and then feeling sorry for myself. A loop that left me dizzy, distracted and hopeless.

I wanted to look in the mirror and not feel such disdain. I wanted to see a woman who didn't let habit blind her to new sources of happiness. A woman brave enough to dare and take risks that make her feel alive.

There was a soft voice inside, telling me I had something special to offer the world, but I had no idea what it was. I blamed my past and I blamed my composition. With a family history of mental illness, I expected to be unstable.

I looked around at the walls I'd built tall with bricks made of shame and regret. Convinced that I'd be seen as a fraud if I tried to change my path; I refused to admit I wasn't happy. I covered my problems with smiles and good times.

I admired people who spoke their minds and said precisely what they meant — and with confidence — knowing that their voices matter in the world. I wanted to find that kind of strength, to express myself without fear and be true to myself.

That became my mission.

I decided to make the world more beautiful by being honest and admitting I didn't feel beautiful or gracious or strong.

I craved a place where I could be peculiar and disheveled. I was tired of trying so hard to look clean when I knew I was dirty.

Flowers *need* dirt to grow.

Instead of asking for my dirt to disappear, I asked for strength to grow in the mud and stand tall in it.

Drawn to books, people and stories about transformation and changing one's life against all odds, I desperately wanted to learn how to heal myself and stop acting like a victim.

This desire gave me the jolt of enthusiasm and purpose that I needed to keep going. I turned to face myself and became fascinated with what I found.

That is when I realized that I could live a different story.

III

Self-discovery

WHERE YOU LOSE YOURSELF

When you've been told, over and over, that you are too much or not enough, it echoes through your actions. Even if you don't consciously accept it, you're sensitive about it, you react to it, and there it has you.

Tired from defending yourself, wilted from suppressing yourself, fighting inner and outer battles that will never bring you peace.

When you need someone's permission to feel how you feel, to be different, to be curved and slanted the way you are, you give them your power. You let them shade your light. Parts of you go missing. Gifts go unused.

When life hurts because you've lost yourself while living it, you think you're too far gone. Living life as someone you don't want to be, seeing no feasible way out, you wonder what would happen if you let it all go.

If you threw up all the words, danced out all the pain, and unleashed all the light.

MORE THAN THEY CAN SEE

The earliest steps of self-discovery are the hardest because we have to admit that we're not doomed and we actually have endless possibilities. Bad genes, bad luck and bad decisions can no longer take the blame.

We have to change the way we think, contradicting every self-defeating thought we've ever had.

My therapist asked me what I liked to do as a child. My first thought was of my mother taking me to the library every two weeks, keeping me stacked with books to occupy me.

Behind my closed bedroom door, surrounded by stories, hope dropped down its hand and I climbed in to be carried away. I discovered worlds that welcomed me more than this one. I fell in love with authors who wrote my intimate thoughts and fantasies without knowing me.

Reading was not only an escape, it kept me rooted in possibility. It was safe to let my guard down in the pages of a book. Words had the power to transform my situation, or at least my experience of it, to make it not only bearable, but meaningful, connected to a larger story. Books defy a certain loneliness of the soul.

Therapy led me to welcome writing back into my life.

With my creative light turned on, I began to see myself differently and share myself more openly. Self-discovery and creativity became intertwined. Writing became my art and the first place in a long time where I felt the courage to show how sensitive I was.

I didn't set out to be an artist or an entrepreneur. I was simply peeling back layers, shedding old skin, trying to find the core of me.

In that process, I found a vibrant soul who was unwilling and unable to hide anymore.

SWEET SOLITUDE

When transformation called, solitude became my portal to peace and creativity. Hours were like minutes and the time alone inspired new ways of thinking. Nothing to explain, no one to put at ease, no one to entertain or impress.

Only when I'm alone does the world make complete sense. No one needs to pay attention to me but me.

During my time alone, I built confidence. I started to understand the world in a different way by taking time to understand myself. So when tough moments came and I was challenged, I could make heartfelt decisions and live from a place of deep knowing instead of imitation.

A close friend's mom gave me *Lessons in Living* by Susan L. Taylor when I was about 21. She saw me struggling, doing all kinds of self-destructive things and she never judged. She knew I was missing a mother's guidance and she told me that my pain would have a purpose.

I wasn't sure of my purpose but a seed was planted when I read these words from the book, "Our fears can immobilize us, make us feel alone and unprotected, lost and confused, unable to see the many trails leading out of the woods. There is always a way out. The way out is within."

I read books by Deepak Chopra, Eckhart Tolle, Iyanla Vanzant and Paulo Coehlo. I meditated on *Lovingkindess* by Sharon Salzberg and *A Return to Love* by Marianne Williamson.

As the lights came on, I had less time for old habits. My world expanded and I distanced myself. Monopolized by transformation, I created my own cocoon.

Self-confidence grows when you set boundaries that allow you to operate on a higher level and you don't allow the world to drain you. Drain might not come in the form of toxic people and meaningless activities. It can come from taking care of others more than you take care of yourself. It can come from pouring out more than you take in and not understanding the generosity that self-love allows.

For example, I had to stop talking on the phone so much.

It was an escape for me to hop on the phone with my girlfriends and chatter away the stress of the day. It was comforting and familiar, but it ate up a great deal of time that I could have used to process what was going on in my life.

When you don't honor your need for physical and emotional space, you are allowing your state of mind to be determined by what the world throws at you.

I had to become selective about when and how I shared myself, realizing that some parts of my old life would have to be sacrificed for me to become the driven woman I had inside of me. I'd have to put my needs first and stop looking for ways to distract myself.

When I stopped spreading myself thin and trying to be everything to everyone, the criticism came rolling in.

Some gave me the cold shoulder. They took my need for space personally and they wanted their resentment to be a punishment to me.

Some rolled their eyes and reminded me of who I used to be. They didn't like my new boundaries and they didn't want their control over me to change.

Some meant well, but continued to expect access that I wasn't willing to give. They treated me the way *they* wanted to be treated, and not how *I* wanted to be treated. They couldn't understand why I wanted to be left alone.

When you don't know who you are, and you don't understand your need for solitude, people's opinions can make you question yourself and think something is wrong with you.

Let yourself be who you need to be, and let others be who they need to be. One person's selfish is another person's self-love. Many of us who are thought to be stuck up or standoffish are actually sensitive and shy — wary of letting too many energies touch us.

Being lost and confused for so long taught me to protect my energy so no one could waste it, abuse it, or redirect it.

I decided to relish my time alone and take in the world at my own pace. When you connect your time and energy to your stability and your peace of mind, it no longer matters what anyone thinks because you know their approval can't save you.

God knows that if I sense the people around me are not on my wavelength, I won't say much.

When I'm at my best — channeling love, not fear — I trust my gut feelings about who to open up to and when.

Alice Walker spoke my life when she said, "She was so quiet. So reflective. And she could erase herself, her spirit, with a swiftness that truly startled, when she knew the people around her could not respect it."

PEACE

To the ones you loved who didn't love you back.

To the hearts you broke when yours was broken.

To the possibilities that turned into regrets.

To the question you were to the answer you are becoming.

Let it all be growth.

Let it all be peace.

FROM A DISTANCE

If I were a recluse, I would not go off into the mountains somewhere to live away from society. I would live in a quiet community with plenty of life around me and I would smile and wave but I'd stay to myself.

I would spend most of my days content with my own activities and adventures. No fear of missing out, I would have a phone but I'd keep it on silent. My social life would consist of quality time spent bonding with the people I love, creating with people I admire, and being at peace with the rest of the world — from a distance.

Reclusive means avoiding the company of other people; solitary. I have to admit that sounds lovely. There is no question that I avoid the company of other people often, but I reject the idea that solitude is selfish.

Does that make me antisocial?

One definition of antisocial is to be averse to the society of others. Another is to be unwilling or unable to associate in a normal or friendly way. I used to throw labels like reclusive and antisocial around without knowing what they actually meant. I viewed them negatively and they are terms I tried to distance myself from. But lately I've been wrapping a question mark around the social patterns I thought I had to fit into.

My mother, who is now a card-carrying recluse, did not shut the world out overnight.

She was once a socially-active working mom and wife who volunteered at school, read beauty and fashion magazines and turned the radio up loud while driving around in her little blue hatchback. She immersed herself in church and volunteered at school, talked on the phone and hosted parties. Her nails were painted bright red and her long legs stretched bare and brown in the summer, leading me through my hand-holding years as I looked on in awe of her.

I like to remember that version of her, before she began to withdraw, like a butterfly morphing backwards, retreating back into its cocoon.

The ways of the world disillusioned her. She spoke of threatening voices in her head, voices that became louder than ours and impossible to ignore. She was increasingly nervous and uncomfortable around people, even family and friends. She stopped offering herself up and participating in family events. She stayed in her bathrobe and isolated herself for days then weeks at a time, refusing to answer the phone or the door. Televisions and radios were silenced.

When the sound of my father and I walking on eggshells disturbed her, she'd say things like:

Who put you up to this? Why won't they let me have any peace?

The people were always watching. The people were ever against her. She became antisocial by definition — averse to the society of others. The transformation was gradual, but it seemed to happen abruptly, like the sun going down at dusk.

Back then I told myself I would never stop engaging with the world and that I'd never isolate myself the way she did; but the older I get and the more of this world I consume, I find myself avoiding contact with people and unknown energies and new environments. I'm sensitive to all of it, just like she was.

She and I share the heavy blessing of being highly sensitive; feeling so much, so easily, so deeply. I'm moody and like to be left alone most of the time, yet I crave connection — a contradiction that has often put me at odds with myself.

PLAYING ALONG

People have always had a distracting effect on me. When I was a little girl, I stared at faces and bodies, looking strangers up and down, intrigued by human nature and how people expressed themselves.

Wide-eyed, I studied the world like I was looking for clues.

Is that family over there as normal as they seem?

Does that woman have angry voices in her head that tell her awful things?

Are there happy people and sad people or are we all a bit of both?

At a young age, I resolved that appearances were important and should be perfected; while authentic feelings, especially troubles, were best kept private.

I didn't set out to become someone that I'm not, but I committed to an image, a version of myself to cling to because everyone else seemed to have one.

IV

Identity

OLD FRIEND

I'm sure you think that I don't think about you, but I do. Every time I meet someone who reminds me of you, I catch myself wondering where I'd be if I'd continued to chase you.

Occasionally, I run into people who mistake me for you and I play along. To start, that means I say yes when I mean no and I agree when I don't agree, but it goes farther. I pretend to have knowledge and interest in things that I don't and I allow people to make me feel small. You've helped me hide for so long and you know me so well, it's been hard to resist the privacy you provide.

I made you up in my mind to escape my reality. I thought if I could make you real, if I could become you, then I'd fake my way to a happy life.

When I let you get away, and the real me started showing up, I punished myself for deviating from the life I thought you would have.

When I partied too much and lost my scholarship, you started to disappear.

When I became a mother before I became a wife, you disapproved.

46

When my poor decisions resulted in financial turmoil for myself and my family, you wanted to die and you wanted to take me with you.

My attention seeking, disregard for responsibility, and refusal to acknowledge the root of my recklessness all left me no choice but to take off the mask of you and take a hard look at the real me.

You were never real.

You were a character I created based on what I thought people wanted me to be.

I even convinced myself that I wanted to be you:

Perfect. Fit in and keep up and never miss a beat. Have-all-the-right-things perfect. Never-admit-that-I-need-help perfect. Friends-approve-of-me-and-family-is-proud-of-me perfect.

Because the alternative was to actually get to know myself and that was too risky. No, I thought, I'd better strive to be accepted, cover my problems, hide my blemishes. Be the good girl they expect me to be.

To this day, I smile to myself when people notice that I'm not you and they look at me differently.

I never wanted to live in the box you kept me in, but I told myself I'd be safer that way. I idealized normalcy and you were the embodiment of that.

Thank you for teaching me who I am not, so I can learn who I am.

Let it all be growth.

Let it all be peace.

THE TRUTH ABOUT THE LIES

We pretend so we can cope.

We pretend so we can fit in.

We pretend to avoid judgment.

We pretend for fun.

Sometimes we pretend because we don't know who we are.

I found that most people didn't want my reality. They only wanted to hear things that made them feel comfortable.

I saw truth telling lead to disapproval, punishment, sadness, and anger. Being the people-pleaser that I am, I lied to keep the peace. I lied to protect people's feelings. I lied to make myself seem bigger, to make myself seem smaller, whatever the situation called for.

Most of all, I lied to guard my secrets and insecurities.

Once you start pretending — telling a story about yourself that isn't true — you feel like you need to maintain that story, keep up the facade. This effort drains your energy, makes you feel like an imposter; you worry about being found out, you run and hide.

But authenticity offers freedom.

It's like a built-in guarantee, but we don't trust it. It guarantees that we are on the right track as long as we are being honest with ourselves and with the world about who we are and who we are not. Carl Rogers said, "What you are is good enough if you would only be it openly."

I remember how it felt to go to sleep at night and wake up each day without my voice.

I remember when I had more friends, but I wasn't truly a friend to myself.

I remember trying to fit in, trying to be different, and finally showing my bare face and being seen.

I remember the first time I spoke my truth and my words unlocked the truth in someone else.

Until we realize how much we are holding back from ourselves, we cannot see how much we are holding back from the world.

CHASING AND RUNNING

I thought I had this self-love thing figured out. After years of being lost and confused, I finally understood that I was responsible for my own life and my own self-perception.

In the words of Ntozake Shange, "I found god in myself and I loved her, I loved her fiercely."

When I opened myself up to this love, I thought my whole mindset would change — just like that. I didn't know about the ongoing work and practice and hunger of self-love. I didn't know how consistently it needed to be fed.

Often we ask for growth but we don't want to go through the lessons necessary to stretch us.

I thought that loving myself and understanding my purpose would make it easier to tear down my walls. This was my dream, to find the courage to do something positive with my problems.

Creative living was the heavenly destination I sought. The promised land. With my inner and outer worlds aligned, I imagined I'd be happy all the time, fulfilled in every activity, and loved and understood by everyone who mattered.

My sensitive, quiet nature wouldn't be a problem, in fact, it would be the source of my ingenuity.

But this evolving purpose, this all-consuming creativity not only enchanted me, it also alienated me.

I still felt like I was chasing something I would never catch.

The chase didn't leave me alone and it didn't come and go. Even in the most euphoric moments — making love, cuddling with my children, laughing with friends — I was thinking about how to find the words, how to tell the story of this deeper vibration, to write my way through my obsessions.

When I couldn't translate my life into works of art fast enough, hopelessness seeped through the vents of my hastily built heaven and I began to backslide.

So close but so far to go, I could see transformation on the horizon, but I didn't feel capable or worthy of it.

No stranger to being a day late and a dollar short, negative thinking was not as easy to turn off as I thought it would be. Knowing better did not necessarily equal doing better. I was still looking for approval and I was still discouraged when I didn't get it.

I said I wanted peace but I kept going in circles, telling myself victim stories that stole my peace away — chasing truth, running from change, chasing truth, running from change.

SELF-LOVE

Self-love is not simply a change of mind, it's a reconditioning that takes practice and commitment. It is learning and unlearning.

Self-love is knowing that you may feel inadequate, unwanted and misunderstood at times but you are more than those feelings and there is more to your story.

Self-love is embracing your extremes, contradictions, weaknesses and blind spots.

Self-love is knowing you are never out of love because the source is inside of you.

CREATIVE MATERIAL

If every day you wake up and insist on the same thought patterns that keep you in pain — condemning yourself for past mistakes, rejecting yourself for not having it all figured out — you are creating a self-fulfilling prophecy of defeat that will stay with you wherever you go.

Instead, travel light. Forgive yourself. Forgive others. Make your story about the process and the overcoming.

If you want to change the way your life is going, change the story you are telling yourself about who you are and who you can be — rebel against your old story.

What have you been through that you gives you a unique perspective and the ability to help others?

This is your struggle.

What is your favorite way to communicate? How can you use this form of communication to share your story?

This is your vehicle.

What type of people do you connect with most naturally, with the least amount of effort or anxiety?

This is your audience.

How can they find you? How do you put yourself out there?

This is your platform.

How have your ups and downs, your wins and losses shaped your life?

This is your story.

What happens when you live out the story your heart wants to tell?

This is your purpose.

When you own your story, you can use it to help people.

Stories allow us to offer up our humanity as a gift.

V

Sensitivity

SMALL TALK

What is your story? What keeps you up at night?

Most people don't expect these types of questions to come from a complete stranger. But this train of thought is more interesting to me than small talk about the weather. If we can't go beneath the surface just a little, then I'd rather not talk.

What drives you? What puts the fire in your bones? How is your heart?

These are the conversations that keep my interest. I like to swim in the deep end.

I seek the stories, the context and layers that make you who you are. I crave soul connections and I'm drawn to creative, honest energy.

I want you to know, I want everyone to know, that I see them and what lies beneath is what matters to me.

Labels bore me. Titles mean nothing. As an idealist, even facts are subjective to me.

If you could see into my brain, you'd find me paying attention to the emotional currents in my environment like who was offended by a comment, who feels uncomfortable speaking but wants to be heard, who is overbearing and needs to be buffered.

Sometimes I'm so busy noticing the energy and the body language around me that I completely tune out of conversations.

As a result, I often feel like I'm floating in a different world than everyone else.

My ideas run my life every day, pulling me here and there, often before I have fully processed the ones from the day before.

I indulge in what is called divergent thinking, where my mind is constantly flowing through stories and associations that only make sense in my own mind, linking unrelated things.

This is the opposite of convergent or critical thinking, the kind that helps you excel on standardized tests, for example.

For so long, I tried to work within categories and definitions. Everything was good or bad or black or white. Rich and poor were only monetary measures. Success had a universal meaning.

These strict guidelines became more and more insensible when my life became too complicated for absolutes and everything went grey.

My life on paper, when regarded without perspective, made me feel like a penny with a hole in it until I started telling myself a different story about my life, my gifts, my pain and my passions. You know, the things that keep *me* up at night.

And that's what puts the fire in my bones — living an inspired life. I find purpose in making art with my pleasure and pain and sharing wisdom in creative ways.

We aren't defined by where we grew up, or where we went to school, or what our parents did or didn't do, or anything else that happens to us or because of us. We don't have to wait until we have it all figured out before we feel worthy of being seen and taking up space.

The facts we allow to empower or diminish us are merely the plot points in the true tales we need to tell. Our real life stories happen in the less obvious, hidden places in our self-conscious where we are processing our experiences and deciding how to respond to what comes our way.

So I ask people about what keeps them up at night and what drives them and what makes them feel happy or smart or sad because I want to know what stories they are telling themselves and on what facts or myths those stories are based.

I want to know who you are when no one is looking. I want to know what you think you have to hide but don't, just this once.

I want to know the part of you that doesn't want to be seen but seeks attention.

So I can smile and say:

I see you. Do you see me?

ALCHEMY

You may be intensely sensitive and your feelings may be easily hurt.

You might wonder why every little thing affects you so much.

But as you learn to accept your empathy and your complex inner world, you will discover a new way to respond to those feelings.

You will become more compassionate and less consumed by other people's quirks and inconsistencies.

You will know that their actions reflect their stories, not yours.

There will come a day when you will be angry or disappointed or sad and still aware that when the fog clears, you've lost nothing.

Because no one can take away your peace unless you give it away.

No one can define you, limit you, stress you, unless you give them permission.

People can throw their broken pieces at you and you can walk away without a scratch.

That is when you will understand that your sensitivity is a strength, not a weakness.

The world needs those of us who can absorb pain, process it, and transform it into love.

There are people out there just like you.

People who value experiences in an introspective way and appreciate someone whose energy helps them slow down and focus.

This is a superpower too — a softer, less celebrated quality — but still relevant and necessary.

Don't overlook the power you have to be a breath of fresh air and awaken feelings of being seen and appreciated in a world where most spaces are full of egos, angst, and competition.

THE WEATHER

It was January and it hadn't snowed at all yet. I told the cashier at the grocery store that this mild winter weather makes me nervous and I hope we don't get crazy amounts of snow soon to make up for it.

It felt so unnecessary after I said it. Of course she knew it hadn't snowed. I didn't need to inform her but I opened my mouth and that is what came out. I never know what to say for small talk.

I do worry about the weather though. I worry a lot, in general.

I worried on my way to the grocery store that day. I worried that I was annoying the cashier by talking too much.

I spend my life distracting myself from my worries, trying not to overthink everything.

Turns out the cashier was not annoyed and she worries about the weather too. She hates snow. She wants to move somewhere warm enough to have no winters at all but then she'd have to deal with hurricanes and tornadoes and earthquakes. She's glad there's been no snow. It's one less thing to make her late for work. We laughed about that.

I left her lane with my groceries thinking about how I liked her energy and our exchange. In my mind, we were talking about something more than the weather.

What I was really saying was:

> I'm content. Things are going well. But I keep looking up at the sky, waiting for it to fall. It's hard for me to relax. The world is way too uncertain. If I let myself get too comfortable, surely I will be reminded of how fast the seasons change.

What she was really saying was:

> I won't be happy until I'm in control with no surprises. I'm just trying to figure where on this earth I can go to find that arrangement. So far, I can only think of places where there are still unwanted situations and I'm still not in control.

If you really listen to the things people say, the chatter we distract ourselves with can be code for:

Help me, see me, I'm scared too.

Instead of worrying, I'd rather use my imagination to look for meaning and truth beyond the surface. I've been scared by shadows enough to know that when you move the light, the shadow transforms into something else.

Overthinking can make little things huge and great things horrible but imagination can also create simple, strangely meaningful moments from everyday things like chatting about the weather with the lady at the grocery store.

LIGHT-HEARTED

We were sitting at the kitchen table.

Talking about the men, the babies, the jobs.

She shared, I shared, she laughed, I laughed.

I made light of things that kept me up at night.

I envied her ease, she seemed so light-hearted.

I wondered if she was happy or just pretending

Like me.

SOFT PLACES

Why can't we talk about sadness?

It's one of those intimate and inevitable things like sexuality. I don't care who you are, part of you is sad, but you might have been trained to be ashamed of it.

Aren't we all tired of pretending? It feels good to be honest about what hurts.

When we allow it, sadness can be a gateway to creativity.

It draws you in and makes you pay attention to its colors. It sparks your imagination and forces you to turn away from the outside world.

We spend so much of our lives worried about how we look and how we perform. Sadness, when we allow ourselves to revel in it, pulls down our walls so we can explore our softest places.

I was an intense kid and I learned early on that it wasn't a cool thing to be, so I did my best to conceal my feelings. But everything stayed with me. I carried not only my own problems around but those of everyone else.

The sunburned, homeless man on the corner with a cardboard sign.

The elderly woman looking wobbly and confused in the grocery store.

Even the murderers in the mug shots on the news — weren't they once innocent babies? What did life do to them?

I thought I was weird for mourning so much, but I needed to take my time and let the grief of human existence flow through me.

Same with joy. Just as I had a deep capacity to explore sadness and pain, I felt intense joy at what others considered to be small things.

I realized that I looked at life differently than many people.

No matter where I was — school, church, or with friends and family — there were things I kept to myself to fit in and go with the flow. I stayed quiet and conflicted about what to do with the sticky sadness that clung even to my happiest moments.

Being highly sensitive is a gift and a challenge. You might feel that you overreact or take things too personally. You may enjoy social interaction and want to get involved in a lot of things but you get overwhelmed quickly.

You might think that you just feel too much.

I saw the world as a place that didn't cooperate with sensitive souls like me.

Tortured by anxious, tragic thoughts, I developed an abusive relationship with life where I tried to hurt myself before it could hurt me, grieving in advance.

How much time you spend thinking about what you *don't* want to happen?

This habit creates a mindset where we're afraid to be too happy because something could be waiting around the corner to knock us down.

Anxiety hinders self-expression, corrupts imagination, steals the moment. It can lock you in your home and in your mind, afraid to talk to people and try new things.

You worry about what you're missing and what people are saying about you.

You wonder why you can't relax, perpetually bracing for the worst.

You worry that you'll never stop worrying.

You're sad because you're worried. You're worried because you're sad.

When sadness loses hope, it becomes depression. I have often wished to be more aloof and not feel so much, because the intensity can easily turn dark.

Heavy emotions need a positive outlet. This is why I write. It's the only way I know to cry without crying and scream without screaming. It soothes me to channel my layers into words. When I write about the things that hurt me, scare me, intimidate me, somehow magically they lose their power — allowing me to feel lighter.

For better or worse, my sensitivity is the core of who I am and all the best stuff I bring to the world comes from this place.

THE FIGHT IN ME

If it's all about winning, I don't want to play. Some people argue and debate for sport. I'd rather be quiet and even misunderstood than use my energy competing with someone, trying to win an argument. It's not worth my energy to convince someone to see things my way if they are decided against it.

Arguments shut me down.

I need time to process and think. My voice may quiver and my eyes may water, both from frustration. I am saturated with flowing thoughts and waves of emotion as I try to find the right words and the right reaction.

Fight or flight. I may shut down and run away or completely lash out, saying the loudest, most hurtful things I can.

When I do lash out it's because I don't understand what is happening inside of me, why I feel so much anger and I don't know what to do with it.

When any part of your consciousness goes unexplored, it has the power to control you. You know you have those moments when you ask yourself: What's wrong with me? Why can't I control myself? Why do I let this person get to me this way?

I've had this script running through my mind from years of being dismissed and manhandled and not speaking up for myself:

Nice girls finish last.

Nice girls get talked over, ignored and underestimated.

Nice girls let people have the last word and they don't stand up for themselves. They do things they don't want to do because they are too nice to say no.

With these thoughts running through my mind, I don't want to be nice, I want to be a force that is not easily crossed. When I lose my temper, it's not just my reaction to the situation, it's also my anger at being triggered in the first place. I resent feeling trapped in an emotion I don't enjoy; I don't want to argue, but I don't want to be a pushover either.

One time I had a client who didn't pay me when she said she would and I suspected she was taking advantage of me. We'd both made adjustments to the timeline and we'd been flexible with each other over the life of the project, but when weeks went by and she didn't communicate or pay me for the work I'd done, the nice girl script got loud in my head and I wrote her an angry email. I'd let those nice-girls-finish-last fears simmer inside of me and I assumed the worst.

When I'm at my best, I'm calm and thoughtful and aware of my emotions without being a slave to them. I'm graceful in the midst of discomfort. I know that I learn about myself from my relationships and interactions with people.

The way I expressed myself to her came from a place of fear, not from love or wisdom, and I was certainly not at my best. While my concerns were valid, I didn't like the fact that I put harmful energy out into the world through my harsh words.

I've been burned by clients before and I stayed quiet and calm and wrote them off as lessons learned. This client caught the wrath that the others were spared.

Sometimes a situation hits a nerve, an insecurity that I have yet to fully acknowledge, and because I haven't dealt with it, I have an emotional, defensive reaction. I go against my instincts, and I do what I think a strong person is supposed to do, or what a tough person is supposed to do, and sometimes that works out and it ends up feeling right, like I stood up for myself, and then sometimes it doesn't.

All I can do is learn from it and remember that I grow more from being me than trying to be some generic form of strong.

My client's reaction was hurt, but gracious, kind and apologetic. I felt terrible for allowing my fears to get the best of me. There will always be someone who will test you. You have to do the work to understand yourself and change how you respond to these tests.

All my life I'd admired fiery women who smacked people down who crossed them. When I began to identify with being a highly sensitive person, that is when I learned that my strength is not in lashing out.

I don't want any applause that comes from snapping, acting out and forgetting who I am. I have no desire to beat, outsmart or punish with my rightness. Instead of who's right, which is completely subjective anyway, I care about the growth.

My whole life people told me I needed to toughen up, but I stayed soft.

I decided that if I was going to learn how to be more forceful, I would find the strength in my softness and be aggressively kind.

Kindness is brave. Kindness requires self-control, conviction and empathy. So when my buttons are pushed, I remember what matters to me.

I don't question if this is an acceptable way to be anymore, if I am too nice or too passive. This is who I am and how I show it.

If you feel the same way, let this be your permission to stop feeling pressured to fight the way other people do. Do the inner work to understand how you think and how you react to contention.

Anger is a sign to reflect inward.

I believe in fighting for what you believe in. Fighting to find meaning in the puzzles of your life. Fighting to get up again and again after falling down. I believe in fighting with honesty and love.

When it comes to trivialities and miscommunications, I rarely find that my anger is stronger than my need for peace. I remember grace and how the world needs more of it and I think: Why shouldn't I be the source right now?

But does this make me — weak? Too nice? Too passive?

Unwanted situations come and go, but my battles are only ever with myself, between my heart and my mind, my old habits and my next level. Over the years, I've put so much energy into explaining my actions and wanting to be understood, but ultimately I am who I am.

I crave a world where people are open and wear their hearts on their sleeves. A world where we know that sincerity heals and we don't need to fight against who we really are.

VI

Shadows

POINTING FINGERS

I rarely, if ever, chime in on celebrity gossip online. The way I see it, celebrities are human beings and it feels weird to pick their lives apart and make assumptions based on the bits and pieces of their lives that we hear about through the distorted lens of the media.

Can you imagine what it's like to live in the public eye like that?

I know it's their choice, but it's still a huge sacrifice, particularly if you're a private person who just so happens to be a celebrity. I've done so many stupid things and have tons of skeletons in my closet, so I prefer to let everyone else have theirs too. I enjoy the art they make and I don't speculate on their private lives.

Gossip sells because there is something gratifying about seeing others make mistakes and struggle. Without an understanding of where this comes from, we find false comfort in taking our minds off our problems by directing our criticism onto others.

Criticism is a huge part of our culture and many of us hide our true selves when we observe the harsh words and judgment all around us.

When we are faced with challenges daily, we can easily find

ourselves holding back because we see how the world will judge us if we fail to deliver.

It takes a lot of courage to live boldly and risk failure in front of people. People do what they do because they are living out their own lives, their own dreams, and the unique lessons they have to learn.

Since I started taking more intentional risks in my life, I've become more sensitive to how I perceive others and the decisions they make.

Who am I to judge, and likewise, who am I to let someone else's judgment stop me?

When I entertain bitter, negative conversations about other people, this vibe stays and poisons my creative spirit.

We must each value our own ups and downs and wins and losses and find meaning in them even if no one else does.

BIGGER

I am not trying to be perfect.

I am trying to love bigger and be more brave.

I am paying attention to what life has to teach me

I want to do better. But I also want to journey in peace, without constant criticism and judgment.

I want to be a soothing refuge for myself.

I try to avoid tripping over the same bump in the road more than once, but it happens. I trip. I fall hard and get bruised.

I'm not ashamed of my bruises anymore. I have lived. I am living. There's no need to hide that. I have scars, each one kissed with acceptance.

If I didn't have these scars I wouldn't know how beautiful they could make me feel.

A THIEF IN THE NIGHT

There was something magnetic about her. I wanted to be her friend. I also wanted to study her, poke holes in her mystique and find flaws.

I saw her wins as my losses and her strengths as my weaknesses.

Everything about her was organic and effortless. I went out of my way to see what she was wearing, what she was doing and how she went about it. My feelings puzzled me as I watched them shape shift in response to her — admiration and respect, resentment and jealousy — she inspired me then put me in a bad mood.

There are three questions that envy loves to ask.

When will it be my turn?

I used to tell myself to be patient. I'd say, Your turn is coming. Blessings are on the way. This mindset kept me envying other people's blessings and overlooking today, in favor of some tomorrow.

Patience is important but it's more than simply waiting for results, resolutions, blessings or anything else. It's about seeing the goodness right in front of you and being grateful in the moment.

Even when you are uncomfortable.

Even when you are uncertain and scared, nervous about what will happen next.

Even when you are working hard and stretching yourself to change your life.

Be patient by embracing the journey for the growth and the love, not for bragging rights or proof of your worth. Be willing to experience everything your journey has to offer and don't try to skip the lessons that come for you.

The alternative is to feel unsatisfied, focused on lack, eyeing what other people have, overlooking the abundance that is available to you in the moment.

Why does everything work out for her and go wrong for me?

Imagine being able to see into everyone's soul. If our insides showed on the outside, would we compare and compete so much? Would we make so many assumptions?

Or would we be able to see clearly that we're all human and complex inside and out?

We'd see the abuse that successful woman had to overcome to get where she is.

We'd see the grief that other woman walks around with every day, all the people she's lost and the sacrifices she's made.

We'd see how much the seemingly confident one dislikes herself and how gentle the mean one used to be before life beat all the hope out of her.

Comparison is everywhere, all the time. But if we look a little deeper, into ourselves and each other, we can see that it's an illusion and we can choose to respond to it differently.

Why do I feel invisible and unimportant compared to other people?

When you feel small, maybe even invisible, it's not a sign that you don't matter. It is a reminder to pay attention, to love yourself, no matter your circumstances or how you happen to feel that day. It has nothing to do with what you think you need from other people.

The longing for attention can sneak up on you, telling you that you need something to happen, a spotlight maybe, a big deal.

Something that proves you are special.

Take time to notice what makes you feel stimulated and alive. You are fully capable of honoring yourself.

When you find yourself waiting for someone to see you or fill you, stop right there, and give *yourself* what you need. When we don't give ourselves this attention, we can find ourselves doing unhealthy things to get some light from someone else.

Our culture teaches us to compare ourselves to each other to determine worth, success, beauty, and status.

It's no wonder we have such a hard time rewiring ourselves from this way of thinking even when we discover that it's hurting us.

But gratitude dissolves envy.

When you eliminate from your mind any resentment of other people's blessings, you can appreciate the abundance around you, even if it's not yours.

Instead of looking at someone else's life to identify your goals, nurture and develop what you have.

Find what's real and inspiring inside of *you.*

UNDERNEATH

When I wake up, it is almost 2 AM and it's raining. The room is completely dark and I feel a moment of panic, trying to remember if I put the baby to bed, put the leftovers in the fridge.

The rain is loud. Is that faulty window leaking? What time did I fall asleep? I jump up and do mama things. In the midst of checking and tidying, the murky emotions of the day come flooding back, unfinished with me.

Every day, I replace negative thoughts with positive ones. I pray away fears. I turn the channel. I change the subject. I redirect my attention. I stay in the light. But sadness builds up under the surface and demands its time with me.

I look around at my life and it seems messy and ineffective.

I look at myself in the mirror and I don't feel beautiful.

And yet I feel so brave.

Proud of all the fears I've faced.

This kind of beauty is different from what I've known before.

It's not pretty.

But it's more real and more meaningful than the surface beauty I once craved.

It gives me the courage to face my darkness with soulful anticipation.

What will I learn from this? How will this spell of sadness resonate in my work and in my life? How will this help me to serve?

Pain always leaves me stronger and more passionate. Wiser for the wear.

INSIDE OUT

For much of my life I've only been as confident as my carefully constructed image allowed. I wanted to look good in person and on paper to make up for how weak I felt on the inside, so I focused on appearances.

The media taught me to compare myself to touched up, perfected images. The more I looked like them, I figured the more acceptable and loved I would be.

It taught me to fix myself to fit certain standards of beauty and that life would be more charmed and happy if I did.

My environment taught me that being pretty was important.

I saw it with my own two eyes: Extra attention. Benefit of the doubt. Get-out-of-jail-free cards. Kindness and consideration.

Most of all, being pretty gave you magical powers like confidence, charm and magnetism and I wanted all of those things.

My mother taught me to invest time in making myself beautiful — caring for my skin and hair, wearing flattering clothes, taking pride in putting myself together and presenting myself. But I missed the reason behind it all.

I believed that I should be doing these things for outside approval: to please my family, to get the attention of a man, to compete with other women, to win favor and feel special.

There was no connection established between self-love and self-care, creativity and self-expression.

I wasn't aware that these beliefs were sabotaging my self-concept and undermining my confidence.

I walked around with my distracting hang-ups and my pride and this unreasonable pursuit of perfection. Obsessing over how I looked, dressing to get any kind of attention I could get, then feeling very uncomfortable with the attention once I got it. Confused. Showing off. Showing too much. Doing too much.

My emphasis on appearance was buried deep in my subconscious, driving my actions, building walls and blind spots and bad habits, leading me down a slippery slope of insecurity.

I knew my definition of beauty needed to change when I got older and it became even more important to me to feel beautiful on the inside. It became a crucial part of my spiritual journey as a woman.

I wanted to know the secrets to inner beauty and confidence and how to feel beautiful no matter what I look like on the outside. Knowing, of course, that this energy would flow out and give me an external presence that would glow.

Stripping down, learning to love my reflection without makeup, without chemicals in my hair and without a closet full of clothes; finding the beauty in all my womanly insecurities has been exactly what I needed to trigger a shift in perception. To appreciate my body for the miracle that it is and start taking care of myself from the inside out.

I needed to shed some old skin and old ideas, redefining myself, for myself.

When we are in tune with our spirits, we feel beautiful on the inside, and we want to express it on the outside. Inner beauty naturally leads to all the magical powers we want — glow, magnetism, confidence, grace.

Without that inside-out dynamic, we find ourselves placing too much emphasis on the external package, excessively proud or ashamed of how we look and acting accordingly.

But a woman who delights in her appearance in order to honor her Creator, her spirit, and her vehicle for expression, that's the kind of beauty I've come to believe in.

VAIN

When I lean in to hug my friend's husband on their wedding day, my reddish-brown bronzer gets all over the shoulder of his tux. He is wearing white. Embarrassed, I continue down the reception line like nothing happened.

My face feels like a melting mask that day. The makeup is piled on heavy because I knew the direct sunlight would be unforgiving on my blemished skin. I tried to camouflage my face so I could look flawless and feel confident.

It never occurred to me that I could feel beautiful with my bare skin and my blemishes. I've had acne-prone skin and scars on my face since I was a teenager. I've been through phases where I wore layers of makeup to cover it up or styled my hair to hide it. Diet changes, vitamins, laser treatments, prescriptions and expensive skincare products — I tried it all.

Maybe for you it's your weight, or your hair, or the shape of your body that has caused you grief and insecurity. The things people say and the images we compare ourselves to combine to create self-consciousness and we dim ourselves, not wanting to draw attention to what we think are flaws.

The way I felt at that wedding stings in my memory because I was so painfully uncomfortable and I let my self-absorption distract me from enjoying a major milestone in my friend's life.

I was consistently trying to look better and thinking about how to fix myself and be prettier — less clumsy, less awkward, more polished.

After that day, it occurred to me that I felt uncomfortable in my skin not because of my so-called flaws but because of my exhausting need to hide them. My refusal to see the sacred in them.

I got tired of that effort. What was the prize? When would it ever be enough? I just wanted to be at peace in my skin and I thought looking flawless would make that happen. I'm not a flawless kind of girl though. I wander. I stumble. I make messes. I have scars.

My youngest daughter used to say, Mommy move your hair so I can kiss your spots. What was a source of inhibition for me was something my daughter loved unequivocally.

Letting my hair go natural made me feel more real. It was a breakthrough. My natural, chemical-free hair reflected my personality and spirit more than relaxed hair. It made me want to see more of who I could be if I stopped altering myself so much.

Soon I fell for the freedom of keeping my face as natural as possible too. Blemishes and all.

I decided to love myself naked, in every sense of the word. Being unashamed of how I look. Letting myself be seen in what I feel is my most beautiful state. Aware that I'm so much more than this skin, this hair and this body. These...spots.

But still thankful for the vessel I've been given and honored to humbly take care of it.

Now I look at my children and I cannot imagine them seeing anything but divine creation when they look in the mirror.

I think about my mom and how I studied everything about her. Growing up, she was the most beautiful thing in the world to me.

I see her and I see my babies so seamlessly blended into my face, my voice, my movements and my consciousness.

How can I find every inch of them unconditionally beautiful and not see that in myself?

SAME GIRL

When I was a little girl, I discovered that I could get attention with my hair. Whether it was good or bad, people often had something to say about it. I was never the best dressed or the most popular, but my hair was a distinguishing characteristic.

From a young age, I learned how to braid it, twist it and roll it up a dozen different ways. Even as I went through adolescent awkwardness, my hair made me feel like I had something attractive going on. I remember the confidence I felt when I had the longest black girl hair in the room. I never outright admitted this to myself or anyone else, but I grew into a woman who was completely dependent on this specific physical feature to make me feel beautiful.

On a Saturday morning in 2016, I woke up feeling desperate. After two days of back to back setbacks that sent me spiraling into what's-wrong-with-me-and-why-do-I-suck-at-life mode, I needed a drastic change. I wanted to see a reflection of the shift happening inside. But I kept seeing the same girl, covering the same things, protecting the same insecurities.

My hair was in a top knot, super dry and thirsty on the outside and damp on the inside after days of neglect. I hopped in the shower to bathe and to cry and I finally took the time to condition and detangle the pile on my head.

I'd been bored with it for a while, but it never occurred to me to cut it.

Because who am I without my long hair?

What will I do without those compliments?

What will make me special?

Something snapped that day. I remember thinking, I should just shave it all off. And for the first time ever, the idea sounded appealing to me.

Funny how sometimes you don't realize how much extra weight you are carrying until something knocks you way down and in your struggle to get back up all you care about is doing away with any and everything that is heavy.

And what you once needed so badly to feel special, you don't even want anymore. It's become a burden. Your priorities have changed, your desires have changed.

This is the moment that you realize you can let go and you can have less and discover that you've gained much, much more.

So I cut it all off.

And it was liberating and it was symbolic.

I let go of all that old energy literally hanging off of me. I wanted to look in the mirror each day and see a reflection of a new me. A woman who is brave enough to make daring changes and have faith through the experiences that stretch her.

I immediately felt lighter.

I'd been acting so pitiful for those past two days, feeling sorry for myself, but standing in front of that mirror with those scissors in my hand and hair all over the floor, I felt empowered.

I stood there thinking about how relentless transformation is.

How it comes for you. How it works its way from the inside out.

How messy it is and how important it is that we endure it.

VII

Simplicity

MORE

Simplicity requires creativity.

Use more of what you already have and be more of who you already are.

SLOWLY

I watch her knocking things over, mumbling under her breath, looking frantic. She's wishing she'd prepared more last night, woke up earlier, made a list.

She is beating herself up for running late (again) and imagining all the funny looks and sideways comments she will receive upon arrival. She's comparing herself, how many kids she has, how far she has to drive, and she's thinking that things are just harder for her.

She finds depth in being troubled. She's an ambitious and obsessive, but open-hearted girl. She knows I'm watching and I can tell my steady gaze unsettles her.

I'm watching to see how she keeps ending up in this place. I'm watching because she is me and it's important that I study myself from a peaceful, open-minded place. Because I want to live mindfully, with a rich and abundant mindset that shows up in everything I do.

But what I want is challenged by who I am. I struggle with maintaining routines. My kids tease me for being forgetful. My friends give me arrival times that are 30 minutes earlier than necessary because they know I need help being on time. I wait until the last minute to communicate important details and this drives people crazy. It takes me forever to build up the energy needed to return phone calls. Making constant decisions and managing emotional roller coasters for my family all day long is rewarding but incredibly draining, and I become exhausted and check out. I daydream and lose time following my wandering mind all over the place.

In the middle of all this, there is a quiet place inside that observes my thoughts, emotions, and actions and it's unbiased and steady.

By tapping into this place, we can see the emotions that are driving our actions and we can channel more patience.

My habit of rushing comes from a fear of going too slow and being left behind. It's a cycle of procrastination and avoidance then ambition and accomplishment. Chasing truth and running from change. Zoning too far out and then zoning too far in. From my quiet vantage point, I see how I condemn myself and question my stability as I go through these shifts.

But I also see that I am more than these passing emotions. With a wider, deeper perspective I can see how much each moment has to offer and I can slow down and focus. Overscheduling, rushing around, being pulled here and there stifles creativity.

Intuitively, I know I need space to breathe and a slow pace for my life to feel good to me, to feel rich. When I don't slow down and pay attention to what I'm doing, I just go on blaming my flaws and feeling out of sorts, which creates a cloud of agitated energy around me.

James Baldwin said, "To be sensual, I think, is to respect and rejoice in the force of life, of life itself, and to be present in all that one does, from the effort of loving to the breaking of bread."

Mindfulness starts with a simple curiosity — looking in at yourself and out at the world — and it evolves into a reverent awareness of each breath, each moment.

Wherever you feel friction in your life, notice what you are resisting and release it, breathe deeply into it.

For me that means cultivating a lifestyle that is unhurried and requires less decisions. For a long time, I deemed this impossible as a self-employed mother with three kids, but now I know nothing is impossible. With love, patience and self-honesty, we can change anything about our lives that we want.

FERTILE

Don't think of what you don't have. Think of the space that you do have.

Wherever you feel lack, there is space.

Space is fertile for creativity.

Use your beautiful mind to create something from what appears to be nothing.

When you do, you'll begin to see possibility everywhere.

SPACE

We didn't give out birthday presents in 2015. My kids went to many birthday parties but we only gave out cards. Prior to that year, I'd avoid a party altogether rather than show up without a gift. Or more often, I'd buy the gift with money that was needed for something else. So that year of attending parties and giving what I honestly could, even if it was just our presence, was a progressive change for someone like me who was used to living beyond her means.

It was a year of learning how to do more with less and how to be frugal. We were challenged to reconsider what we do, how we do it, what we spend and why we spend it. It felt weird, but good weird. The mission was to eliminate the false to create more room for what's real.

I donated and threw away almost forty garbage bags of clothes and household items throughout that year. Some things I had to sneak out when there was no one home to stop me. There were still unopened boxes from when we moved into our house ten years ago. When I threw them all away, the house immediately felt bigger.

I got rid of furniture we didn't need, I repurposed and rearranged, and I made sure everything we kept had a specific place to go. The goal was to create a cozier, more inspiring environment.

Having more space and less stuff has become incredibly important.

I've had to release my old assumption that more stuff would bring more happiness and satisfaction. If I want to live slowly and savor my experiences, I need to protect what is meaningful to me and let the rest go.

For years, I blindly spent myself into debt and stress because I didn't want to miss out. My triggers were everywhere – television, social media, magazines, billboards, even just casual conversation when relaxing with friends. To break the spell, I knew I had to figure out what was driving this anxious pursuit of more, more, more.

Buying things was a vice that gave my ego tangible evidence that I was worthy. It calmed my anxiety about being left behind and being irrelevant. Having less stuff requires more individual character.

We live in a competitive society, where our possessions and our appearances are a big part of our status. Some of us spend beyond our means and overindulge to maintain this so-called status and keep up with the insatiable material world. As a result, we stay surrounded by fluff and filled with a false sense of worth.

I grew tired of being surrounded by clutter, spending money on more clutter and never being satisfied. I realized I was trying to fill a void that couldn't be filled that way.

To face my anxiety and understand what it's trying to teach me, I have to clear and refresh my mind, body, spirit and surroundings. I have to create space, even when it seems there is none.

Creating space is not just about having and spending less, it's also about absorbing less.

"You need more color. You're such a vibrant person. You should brighten things up."

"You should start a book club!"

"Why aren't you on Snapchat?!"

"You should check out what such and such is doing with her business. She made six figures in her first three months."

Advice and ideas are helpful until they aren't. Even the best intentions can lead to overwhelming, distracting commentary that turns into more clutter. To stay on your own path, with your own pace and style, you have to manage your energy and what you allow to influence you.

When I let too much in, I feel uncertain and ineffective. Either I've said yes to too many things and the projects that matter most to me are suffering or I've made too many impulsive decisions and my head, my space, and my schedule have become overcrowded. When there is no room for stillness to process what's happening and how I want to respond, I'm no good. I get nervous and cranky and I start shutting down.

More does not equal better. But since that is what we hear so often, those of us who prefer a slower pace may feel we need to force ourselves to keep up. I haven't always known what I want, how I want it or how to get it. I didn't know that sometimes growth is less about changing yourself and more about being creative with who you already are.

I didn't know that I could push back at the world and say, This is how I work and I need to take my time.

Or that I don't need to jump on every bandwagon to stay relevant.

Or that my kids would learn more from seeing me handle my fumbles gracefully than seeing me pretend to be perfect.

I certainly didn't know that being honest about my clusters of chaos would help and not hurt my relationships and career but it has. I do my best work, my best loving and mothering and living, when I come to the table as my natural, stripped down self, with as few bells and whistles as possible.

By giving yourself the space you need, your emotions aren't so tied up with marginal things and it's easier to focus on what matters. Keep refining and redirecting yourself as you see fit. Do what feels good to you, even if it will take a long time, require a lot of change, or be off-putting to others.

You might be convinced that your needs are impractical or unreasonable, but I believe that we have the instincts we have for a reason. It's part of our purpose to experiment and discover how to work with ourselves the way God made us. Don't cling to any ideas, habits or piles of stuff that aren't working for you anymore.

CHOICES

My wardrobe consists mostly of white, black, grey and tan. I love color but I don't like having too many choices. There's a lot going on in my head, so I like my wardrobe to be plain. It soothes me.

Now that my hair is natural and free and my clothes are simple, I recognize this person I'm becoming. I notice her when no one else does. She's been in there all along and it feels good to finally see her express herself. While I embrace my plainness now, I once thought it was something I needed to fix.

As I decluttered my life, I gave most of my clothes away and started building a capsule wardrobe, refining my self-care routines, developing a simpler, more nutritious diet.

My reverence for the simple has resulted in several guiding principles that keep me from slipping back into old ways:

Capsule everything. Less clothes. Less jewelry. Less makeup. Discovering the bare necessities that make me feel like myself, add value to my life and nuance to my aesthetic. More time, space and energy to shine without fluff that just makes me feel awkward.

Simple abundance. Creating more space and uplifting energy in my mind, my home and surroundings. Simplifying my schedule. Spacing out my obligations. Releasing the need to be everything to everyone. Letting go of negative thought patterns. Making sure everything that takes up space serves a purpose of function, nourishment, play or inspiration.

Creative self-care. Less store-bought products. More natural and homemade. The process of researching, experimenting and making my own products and regimens serves as a creative outlet. Discovering natural solutions makes me feel more resourceful in all aspects of my life and boosts my confidence.

Cultivated certainty. More yes, more no, less maybe. Lingering decisions make me nervous and distracted. Trusting my intuition and owning my decisions creates the energy needed to move forward confidently, ready to accept the results of what I do.

Social mantras. Before I go into social environments, I set my mind on being myself and not giving into intimidation, inadequacy or irrational fears. I tell myself that I am enough, I am present, I am safe and I am grateful.

Savor sensuality. Prioritize pleasure. Escape from stress and welcome sensation through touch and movement. Make stretching and dancing everyday necessities.

My interest in minimalism started with me feeling overwhelmed by clutter. Mental, emotional, physical, and financial. It took me years of stubborn effort to accumulate it and I know it will take me years to clear it out and maintain the space I need. Even this ongoing process serves as creative material.

AWKWARD

On a phone interview with someone I deeply admire, I started the discussion with a laid back energy like I was having a chat with a friend. As the minutes passed, I got worked up as if I'd taken a stimulant that kicked in halfway through the call. My thoughts went into overdrive and nerves started taking over. I couldn't say anything without stuttering and repeating myself.

I was frazzled. I struggled to provide straightforward, concise answers to questions that should have come easily to me, having answered them dozens of times before. Long gone was the calm, be-your-self-ness that I felt when the interview started. When the call ended, I hung up feeling uneasy. When I replayed the interview in my mind, I was sure I'd ruined my chances.

This is nothing new. I geek out when I'm excited or really inspired and once I'm geeked I have trouble expressing myself. I blurt and babble and say a lot of words that don't make sense together. My thoughts and my mouth disconnect. Then I feel weird about it and that just intensifies the problem.

It's scary to surrender to this zone in front of people I don't know intimately but that's what art is, isn't it? Showing your soul? Being vulnerable?

Wherever you feel friction in your life, notice what you are resisting and release it, breathe deeply into it.

I struggled on this call because I tried to hold myself back when I got excited. I became self-conscious about my words and how they would be perceived. My mind tries to distract me when my heart takes over. My heart is confident and knows its truth. My mind has its doubts. They battle with each other — one wanting to be sincere, the other wanting to be wanted.

But I would rather embrace the awkwardness of being candid and free flowing, than settle for the awkwardness of a blocked heart.

To vibrate higher, we have to let our hearts speak and not get distracted by how we look or sound or what people think of our expression. It amazes me that I can write the most touchy-feely things, but when it comes to speaking them, I still get tongue-tied.

In the aftermath of that call, I had to accept the mixed feelings and come home to myself. Remembering that I've made big changes in my life to allow me to be open-hearted and joyful about the work I do. Work that requires me to tap into this shameless place without having to water myself down.

I didn't choose this journey so I could waste energy wondering if I'm too happy, too intense, too excited, or too idealistic. With every experience, my only goal is to show up as myself, channeling love, not fear.

VIII

Alignment

MIRACLE

Something has been calling you, trying to carry you away.

It offers no guarantees but it makes you feel sensitive and warm and alive.

You look at it but you won't touch it.

You pretend you don't hear it.

What your heart knows and is trying to tell you is this:

You already are everything you dream to be.

You only need to act on it.

ONE THING

What is that one thing you know you must do?

That rule you must break. That adventure that calls to you. The curiosity you just have to pursue. What is it?

In 2013, I knew the one thing I had to do was keep writing. I needed to give myself the chance to see what would happen if I didn't hold anything back. Fully expressed with no apologies.

I wrote in my journal:

I want to write my way into more opportunities and experiences that need my voice. I want my story to help someone.

Whatever it is you want for your life, you have to admit it and then you have to keep giving yourself to it and choosing it over and over. You have to answer when it calls you.

Next to my family and friends, writing is what I love most about life. It's the thing that gives me the most magic and hope. My whole courtship with writing has been like falling in love with my best friend, the one I never thought would turn out to be the love of my life.

Many times I've taken writing for granted. I've neglected its needs, kept secrets from it and fought with it. But all the breaking up and making up has only made me more in love.

What is that choice you know you must make?

Make room for what your heart wants and listen to what it has to say. Beneath the emotional obstacles we set up, we know what we need to do or at least what we need to *stop* doing to reach our next level. We know the choices we need to make.

Your next level could be a healthier, more honest relationship with yourself or your partner.

It could be forgiving someone and taking the weight of resentment off your back.

A new job. A new city. A total lifestyle change.

A story you need to tell. A cause you need to speak up for.

You can deny and resist the blessing or you can choose to receive it with open arms.

MAGIC POTION

My friend was gushing about a miracle in a jar that she'd discovered: a new product that promises to speed up hair growth. She's forever looking for potions and spells to make her hair grow, but she puts heat in it every day, doesn't deep condition or wrap it up at night. Essentially, she doesn't want to do the work to keep it healthy.

There's a disconnect here. Everything has a price. It's up to each of us to determine if what we think we want is worth that price.

I've struggled with this because I love to write, but the business side of promoting and expanding my work has been painful for me. My career — specifically, my desire to write for a living — has forced me to rise to the occasion.

How many times have you given up an endeavor because it seemed too complicated?

Not only have I given up, but I can recall many times where I didn't even start. I didn't want to expose what I didn't know and I didn't want to make costly mistakes. Afraid of the risks, I psyched myself out of the rewards.

Are you dreaming about expressing yourself in new ways but waiting until you feel comfortable?

You might think that looking for your own special miracle in a jar is doing the work. Sure, it's lovely when opportunities fall into your lap, but without the right attitude, a high level of dedication and a willingness to be uncomfortable, the good fortune will not be sustainable.

CREATIVE

Another friend of mine once wrote:

"This is the instant where everything that has been out of focus suddenly becomes clear; the moment when you realize that all the things you thought you couldn't change are indeed different; the day you look around and your surroundings are new — the same people, places and things aren't there anymore — the moment when you can tell that you're just not the "you" that you thought you were."

This was the introduction to a website she and I created to provide inspiration and empowerment for women. Working on this project with her gave me my first taste of spiritual and creative fulfillment as an adult.

As much as we like fancy titles and credentials, a meaningful life can't be captured on paper.

It takes a very personal and intimate discovery of self to make life truly fulfilling. This can't be taught in a classroom and it can't be learned from within a comfort zone. For most of us it takes some missteps and disappointments to find the way home.

No one can dictate what will work for you. I was taught that college is the answer, then graduate school, then marriage, then children, then a safe and secure retirement. This is the good life that was ingrained in me and seemed so attractive when I was growing up. Then I grew up and realized that I would have to find my own yellow brick road.

Do you think of yourself as a creative person?

How you interact with people, how you solve problems, how you express yourself — all of these things are products of your creativity. Your life is your art.

Do you think of yourself as adventurous?

The places you go, the u-turns you make, the experiences that you seek out — all of these things are part of your adventure.

If you have a habit of telling yourself that you are not a creative person you are selling yourself short.

For me, it was a defense mechanism. I didn't feel like I had anything particularly unique to add to the world, so I told myself in a most repetitive, self-defeating fashion that I was not creative.

Commonly, the harsh realities of our lives smack us so hard that we stop using our imaginations.

But didn't we all start off as curious children who were more in touch with imagination than reality?

We didn't understand all of the complexities going on around us, so we created our own stories.

Enter adulthood, and we keep telling ourselves stories but they become more and more negative and limited.

We stop taking chances because we're afraid to fall down, afraid to be rejected, afraid to be vulnerable and do things differently. Afraid to make our own rules. Afraid to create something meaningful and authentic. Afraid, afraid, smothered and afraid.

HARD THINGS

Changing your life is hard, but we can do hard things. We can change our minds and make different decisions, we can unbind ourselves.

The smallest can become the biggest. The faintest can become the loudest. But we have to be patient, test the faith and trust the slow knowing.

We must make our attempts and celebrate every promise that we keep to ourselves. Open-hearted, brand new. Bravely creating the glorious out of the mess.

There is power in letting yourself be as pure and extreme as you truly are even when your mind is telling you that people will judge you. There is no way around it. To be free, you have to let yourself be seen.

Before you ever hear me say — It all just fell into place! — you will hear the honest truth about how it first all fell apart.

In 2009, I started blogging as a hobby.

I had two kids at the time, a demanding job, no creative outlet whatsoever. A whole part of me was lying dormant while the rest of me was rushing through life in survival mode. Blogging sparked a light in that dormant place and it's only grown since then.

Looking back at my writing from those early days is embarrassing. But we all have to start somewhere and often that is precisely where we get stuck. We're scared to start because we don't know what we're doing and we feel inadequate.

But sometimes something clicks so perfectly, scratches an itch, gives us something we've been missing in such a way that we feel compelled to deal with the discomfort and keep going. That is what blogging did for me. It filled a void that I'd been trying to get other people — my man, my family, friends, my corporate career, my possessions — to fill for me.

2012 was a pivotal year.

I decided to start taking my blogging and writing seriously and to see what would happen if I didn't quit and sabotage myself. That was the year I got my first paid freelance writing gig, writing for a beauty and haircare company's blog. That is when I started to believe that writing was meant to be more than just a hobby for me.

Things happened quickly after that, but it didn't feel quick at the time. It felt like a slow, steady process like losing weight or paying off debt. By July 2013, I'd quit my job and was in the thick of creating my own products and services. I was all in.

I walked away from a career that paid me well and gave me stability, but made me feel like a stranger to myself. I have been up and down and all around since then, but I have never looked back. It's been worth every sacrifice.

Blogging introduced play and creativity back into my life. It gave me a reason to write every day, to look at life as a source of inspiration and not a source of fear or struggle.

It allowed me to tap into a part of my being that I didn't have the courage to express verbally. That became my escape. The place I was willing to be uncomfortable and determined and vulnerable for, so I could make it my livelihood.

I had bold and naive ideas about how my entrepreneurial journey would go.

I expected my first book to sell hundreds and my second book to sell thousands.

I expected schools and organizations to ring my phone off the hook and hunt me down to come speak for them.

I expected to hit publish and like a magic spell, my life would change, money would come pouring in and I would have a wait list of clients trying to work with me. I thought, if I build it they will come.

It didn't happen that way.

Book sales were decent for the first couple of months then fell off. Lots of coaching clients reached out to work with me but were unpredictable, changing their minds and canceling appointments and not completing the assignments.

My partner lost his job unexpectedly. No one was hunting me down to come speak for them. I didn't have a solid plan for what to do if my book sales didn't meet expectations. My courses sold well, but not residually.

All the failed attempts I'd made in my life came charging through my mind, knocking down my courage and my certainty.

I realized why entrepreneurs should have a business plan. Why marketing and profit planning are crucial. Why you have to diversify and strategize. Why I can't just be a creative butterfly and I have to actually learn how to be a smart business woman.

In many ways, I was failing.

The bills were piling up. My savings were dwindling and my credit was suffering. My disappointment was palpable, but I was also learning from my mistakes. I was loving my work, building wonderful new relationships and getting positive feedback on my books and courses.

I was helping people. I received emails every day from women saying my words woke them up and changed their lives.

This creative journey revealed a new woman to me.

One who doesn't hide from scary things like failure, discomfort, sacrifice and criticism. A woman who can do hard things for the right reasons.

I love this new woman. I love how she has embraced minimalism and simplicity and how she's learning that abundance is not limited to how much money is in her bank account. I love how she wakes up every day excited to work. How she has redefined failure and is using it as a platform for success.

This is just a part of my story.

My faith is my rock. I have no regrets and no doubts that I've chosen the right path for me. I hold my love for the work in my hands, making sure I don't drop it, no matter what is thrown at me.

When you face disappointment or failure, this is not a reason to quit. This is when it's time to shed that skin and transform into a more experienced, more aware version of yourself.

If you are called to do something out of your comfort zone,

you will fail — at some point.

But you will also bounce and fly and find kindred spirits and you will laugh and cry and feel alive and you will create beautiful things that make you proud. You will see miracles happen.

You will have days that are hard and wonderful and true.

You will be vulnerable in more ways than you ever imagined.

You will cry tears of joy and effort.

All the things you thought you couldn't do will indeed prove difficult — but not impossible.

WHERE YOU FIND YOURSELF

When your shame becomes a story of overcoming, you know you've turned a corner.

When you clear your throat and stand on trembling legs and speak your truth, you sleep soundly at night.

You look forward to tomorrow, as unruly and uncertain as it may be, and you align your steps with your heartbeat, a rhythm that was once muted.

IX

Shamelessness

FREE

A little self-righteous and sheltered.

A little rebellious and unruly.

Meet the good girl who breaks the rules to stay free.

A part of her hides yet craves to be seen.

There's a wild in her heart that she calmly obeys.

Watch the storm she creates when her words start to rain.

SHARP EYES

I was out promoting my first book, speaking at a book club
meeting, and I met a woman with sharp eyes and a firm handshake
who didn't like the book at all.

She said, What was it about? The whole time I couldn't figure out
where it was going and what was the point.

She was the first one to speak and she had a lot to say. I was
hoping everyone didn't feel this way, but I'd prepared myself to not
take anything personally.

I was so focused on being open-minded in the moment that I
didn't really have an emotional reaction to her comments until
later. Most of the women in the book club had positive feedback. I
was thankful for that. The book offers up a part of me that I don't
share with most people and to have it embraced was encouraging.

That night when I got home and was able to be alone, the anxious
thoughts kicked in.

I thought about the lady with the sharp eyes and I replayed
everything she said in my head. She wasn't rude at all, she just
didn't get it. Floating around just beneath the replay loop, I held

these questions in my mind:

How could I have done better? Did I rush it? Should I have gotten more feedback before I published? Should I try to write more like this person or that person?

It didn't matter that all the other women loved it, all I could see were those sharp eyes and all I could hear were her detracting comments. Doubt and confusion built up as I let all my energy flow to these lurking thoughts.

Just above all of this, waiting for me to get there, was a higher understanding.

I thought about Sharp Eyes and how I felt sitting there faced with her disapproval. I realized that I could choose to look at this and any rejection objectively without attaching so much emotion and personal drama to it.

Sometimes we turn outer rejection into self-rejection. Thinking small, we turn on ourselves. But thinking big, we can turn more into ourselves, not allowing criticism or praise to distract us from what we have to say.

When you pour your heart out and think you've shared something special but you don't get the response you want, take pleasure in your own expression.

WORTHY

Have you ever wanted something so badly that you dread it?

Have you ever pushed away the very thing you want most, the very life you want most, because deep down you don't believe that you can have it?

You've romanticized it and your expectations have gotten so high that you are afraid you'll ruin it. You don't know what you will have to give up to get it. It seems unattainable so you pretend you don't want it. You talk yourself out of it. You see it coming and you run. All of this is disguised in a common escape:

I'm not ready.

You're scared of the life you want but rather than admit that, you say you're not ready. You want to feel deserving and capable but you don't, so you stay where you are.

Sometimes we say we're not ready but what we whisper is:

I'm not worthy.

If you're driven by the sneaky belief that you're not worthy, then your actions will reflect that and you won't be open to receive.

I know I want a quiet life.

Deep intimacy.

Belly laughs.

Soulmates.

Happy tears.

Endless curiosity.

Fulfilling work.

Inspiring play.

I want to add crazy amounts of love to the world with the things I create. In order to have these things I want and live life this way, I have to know I'm worthy.

What is it that *you* want?

You may not know why you want it or how much it means to you until you go after it. You don't know what the process will look like, how it will affect you or how you will affect the world by pursuing it.

You won't always get applause, acceptance, apologies or understanding from other people. But you can be sure that you want what you want for a reason. Stay focused.

GROWING

It doesn't matter how old you are or how much you accomplish. Just when you think you are grown, life will shake you up and make you feel childish and inexperienced.

There is always some unsettling newness to grow into because you don't know how each season will affect you until you experience it.

You have to face what you don't understand, with your eyes wide open, and pay attention to what's happening even when you're feeling vulnerable and scared. These wide open feelings just let you know that you are being called to grow beyond where you are.

I tried running from newness and avoiding growth for a long time but I began to suffocate. I moved on and thought I'd let that strategy go for good. But I still find these hidden areas of my life that I have yet to study with any consistency or willingness. Parts of me, conflicts within me, that are buried deep and don't answer when I question because they've been ignored and excused for so long.

I'm ready to clear that space for other things.

I've been relishing my stillness and sitting face to face with these secrets.

I'm paying attention to what hurts, what doesn't fit, what needs to be released. I'm making long overdue changes and giving up habits I've clung to for as long as I can remember.

I'm scared to fail, but I am more afraid to continue to let these things hold me back.

Growing up is a lifelong thing and there are cycles. I know how it feels to fall down and get up many times and to try your hardest to do so without everyone noticing.

To sit on the floor in a puddle of tears and say, I won't let this happen again and I won't do this to myself again, only to find yourself back in that same puddle weeks later.

My cycles have taught me to focus beyond the fear, to the other side of it, where wisdom lives.

I'm going through this season like any other season, with a humble spirit, accepting that there is room to grow and it is going to be uncomfortable. But growth becomes less overwhelming when you have a creative outlet that helps you connect with people who are going through similar things.

VULNERABILITY

There are people out there just like you.

But you have to show yourself to find them.

Once you build up your courage and decide to speak up or put something creative out into the world, it may take a while for you to find your people but be patient.

There will be days when you think everything you have to say has already been said. It will feel strange to keep pushing, but do it anyway.

The difference between being shy/insecure and being quiet/powerful is the conviction. You can be quiet and still persistent.

Perhaps you don't talk as much or as loud as others, but your purpose is just as important.

Perhaps you communicate in other ways, through art or service. The vehicle doesn't matter, as long as you express yourself through the way you live your life.

When I published my first book, I might as well have posted a nude photo of myself online. I had to sit with this discomfort, accept it and grow from it.

Rejection is a tough lover, but we need tough love sometimes. We need to be told no and we need to be challenged and see ourselves become more brave and resilient with each rejection.

When you're afraid to fail, you avoid any situation that could end with your feelings getting hurt. But living that way turns out to hurt the most.

Little by little, we have to give ourselves experiences that strip us down and tell the world who we are. It's not about whether they like it or not, it's about how much we like ourselves for finding the courage to do it.

Train your mind to care less about what the masses think and focus on the attention of your supporters, the people who feed your creative energy and give you life. When you write, picture yourself writing to them. When you draw, sing, make, design — picture the people who need your message and how they will receive it.

Even when you're uncertain and you think you're not ready, show up and let yourself have an experience and grow.

Don't talk yourself out of it because you can't guarantee the result.

Life rewards courage.

WHAT YOU ALREADY HAVE

Your definition of a good life does not have to look the way anyone else thinks it should. Whatever feels right for you, whatever aligns your inside with your outside, that's what you should spend your time doing.

Our culture is so obsessed with more, more, more. Go, go, go.

This is not all bad all the time. But we have to be careful. More knowledge, more growth, more abundance. Yes.

More awareness, more experiences, more hard work. Yes!

But sometimes we get twisted up in this, thinking we need to acquire more, be more, do more in order to be worthy.

Effort is important. And stretching. And going beyond your usual — often. But what I also know is that your stretching should be unique to you and my stretching should be unique to me and it should feel good. Painfully good, but good.

I've done the thing where I've stretched myself to accomplish goals that were meaningless to me and while I did learn from those experiences, there is nothing like purpose and knowing that the stretching is allowing you to reach places you truly want to go.

How many times have you tried to comfort yourself by acquiring more of something?

More money, more accomplishments, more shiny things, more attention?

I spent my whole life trying to acquire things to feel better about myself and it never worked for more than a few minutes. Once I acquired the thing I just had to have, I was already thinking about what else I wanted.

Now I just need this...

I'll be happy when I have this...

I can relax once I accomplish this...

I still want more. But now I want more of what I already have.

I want to see the things that are tucked away, hiding in my blind spots. I want to see what I'm keeping from myself, what I'm ignoring, what I'm not valuing. I want to explore more of my curiosities and ideas. I want to be more resourceful and innovative. I want to expand my comfort zone and stretch more into my growth zone, to the parts of me that I've seen and felt and flirted with but never gone all the way.

Why do we forget that we're enough?

As often as daily sometimes, we forget. Like when we are met with a piece of bad news. A reminder that our lives are not perfect and there are things we don't deal with or handle well at all. And just like that, we may forget that we're still enough and have so much to be grateful for.

Some days, I focus on all the undone things and all the uncertain things in my life and sure enough, I keep finding reasons to feel lacking.

I become a magnet for problems I don't want to deal with, my eyes glaze over and there I am lost in this trance of inadequacy. Everything I set my eyes or my mind on is suddenly in trouble or it's half empty or it's broken.

Louise Hay said, "I don't fix my problems. I fix my thinking. Then my problems fix themselves."

In those difficult moments, I've forgotten that neither my joy, my worth, nor my purpose are defined by my circumstances. And my problems don't hurt me for no reason, they stretch me. They help me see those blind spots, the things I'm ignoring and not valuing.

If my comfort zone was a place where I would beat myself up and perpetuate my own negative habits, then my growth zone is a place where I calmly take a step back and observe what's happening without judgment and without fear.

Instead of panic, more patience.

Instead of hopelessness, more faith.

Instead of complaining, more stillness, more courage.

Now I know I've always had this courage, but was unaware of it. I had to stretch within myself to find it.

I ask myself: What else? How far? How strong can I become?

Because all things are possible with God. I know that. And I want more of what I was made to be. More of what I already have. More of who I already am. Naturally.

X

Writing Guide

THE PRACTICE

They say that actions speak louder than words, but I've always been able to express myself better in writing.

Through writing, I can take my time and fully express myself. Talking, on the other hand, is hit or miss for me. Sometimes my mind and my mouth don't communicate or one moves faster than the other. I get distracted by who I'm talking to or who is looking at me.

Oh, but writing. With no one staring in my face, I can say things that I haven't been brave enough to say out loud or even admit to myself.

Once I write it, it's much easier for me to find my way to saying it. It's a viable confidence plan for those of us who need a little help when it comes to revealing who we really are.

Also, life moves at a quicker pace than I do, so I value the ability to slow down and observe the world and my experiences at my own pace and in my own way.

The practice of writing is a road you can pave to keep you connected to the divine voice inside of you. It's a gift that way.

Many of us think of gifted writers as only those who have a clever or poetic way with words, but it can be a gift for anyone who is willing to be vulnerable through it.

My daughter recently asked me, What is your favorite thing about writing?

My answer was that my problems aren't problems when I'm writing, they are creative material. It's an escape and yet it's a way to find solutions too.

Sometimes we can't immediately change a circumstance, but we can adjust our mindset to find peace in a storm or a lesson in a setback.

Writing is a valuable pathway to self-discovery. It can't change the past or the future but it can change how you deal with it.

––––––––––––

A huge part of writing is listening. Many of us don't truly listen to ourselves. We feel. We think. We react.

Listening to yourself takes practice, patience and stillness. In this way, writing can be a meditation. We come to the page seeking peace and understanding of the deeper truth within in our stories.

Ask daring questions in your writing and expect that with consistency and diligence, the answers to those questions will reveal themselves to you.

I don't mean asking: Why me? What's wrong with me? When will it be my turn? Those questions assume lack and are not productive.

Ask open-ended, open-hearted questions like: Why do I keep going back after he hurts me? Where does my anger come from? What am I lying to myself about?

Somehow, by putting these soul questions in writing, the answers begin the journey of finding their way to us, but we have to be open to receive them and then be brave enough to act on them to make our lives better.

INNER CHILD

When you were a child, how did you like to spend your time?

What was your favorite way to engage your imagination?

Which public figures did you idolize and want to be like when you grew up? Who in your personal life did you look up to? What traits do the people you admire have in common?

What did people tease and praise you for? What did you become self-conscious about due to being teased?

What kind of praise did you become accustomed to receiving?

What made you feel inadequate and what made you feel special? Recall specific situations and how you felt.

How has that little girl evolved over the years? What is your image of her as she has progressed through life? What story have you been telling yourself about her?

What do the people in your life expect from her? What do *you* expect from her?

WHERE YOU ARE

Where are you right now in your life and how did you get here?
What decisions led you here? Were those decisions driven by faith
or fear?

In what ways do you feel stuck? In what ways do you feel free?

In what ways is your life not going the way you want or the way
you thought it would?

What options and possibilities do you have available to you?

What obstacles do you see between where you are and where you
want to be?

What do you look forward to in your life right now and what do
you dread?

In what areas of your life are you doing what's expected of you
instead of what you want for yourself?

What is preventing you from recognizing your gifts, expressing
yourself authentically and living the life you say you want?

SELF TALK

What do you need to admit to yourself right now? What are you hiding, covering up and distracting yourself from?

What negative thoughts and language do you repeatedly say to yourself?

What damage has come from these negative thoughts?

What secret, hard-to-admit beliefs do you have about yourself and what you are worthy to receive?

What do you need to STOP, START, and CONTINUE saying to yourself to improve the quality of your thoughts?

What do you worry about most often?

What do you pray about most often?

Why is it hard to release negative thinking?

SPIRIT

How would you define your approach to spirituality?

Do you believe that you are divinely guided and protected?

Do your actions align with that belief?

What do you believe you were created to do in the world?

In what ways is your inner world aligned with your outer world and in what ways is it not?

How well do you recognize your intuition (i.e. Higher Self, Holy Spirit, divine guidance, etc.) and how much do you trust it?

BODY

Write five things you love about your body. Why? Does your appreciation come from your own opinion or from the opinions of others?

What parts of your body need the most love? In other words, what areas have you hidden, deprecated and loathed?

In what ways do you honor your body and in what ways do you dishonor it?

If your body could talk, what would it say?

When in your life have you felt the most beautiful? Why?

What role has physical appearance played in your willingness to speak up, use your voice and be seen?

LETTING GO

What does it mean to you to surrender?

Recall a time in your life when you needed to let go and move on and you didn't. How did that turn out for you? What did you learn from it?

In what areas of your life are you fighting for control? What do you need to release?

Who do you need to forgive? Are you willing? Why or why not?

What forgiveness do you need to give to yourself?

How will you know when you have truly forgiven? What will be different?

THE REAL YOU

How do you describe you truest, most uninhibited self?

Do your friends and the people you spend most of your time with know you for the real you or are they more familiar with your representative? How would they describe the real you?

Do you feel misunderstood? Do you feel supported? How does (or doesn't) your inner circle inspire you to be more of yourself?

What different roles do you play day to day and how often do you get to relax into your natural self?

What parts of yourself do you suppress and what parts do you accentuate in your different roles?

What makes you feel whole?

PATTERNS

How have your family and/or childhood experiences affected the patterns you see in your life?

What patterns do you want to continue and which ones do you want to end?

What new patterns do you want to create?

Who else will benefit from changing the negative patterns?

FEELING YOURSELF OUT

How do you like to spend your time? What comes naturally to you?

What makes you feel strong and capable? What do people ask you for help with?

What makes you feel energized and useful? What service do you like to provide for people?

What positive qualities do you have that you tend to play down or diminish?

In what environments do you feel most comfortable to freely express yourself?

Who are "your people"? In other words, what kind of people do you like to be around and share ideas with?

In what ways can you insert more of your personality into the things you already do?

PASSIONS

Where do you feel an urge to help? What issues in the world tug at your heartstrings in a deeply affecting way?

In what ways can you combine something you love with something you are good at? For example, I love to write and I'm good at helping women find meaning and creative healing through the written word. Your turn.

In what ways can you combine something you love with something you have overcome? For example, I love to write and I love to help women who have struggled with self-love and emotional health. Your turn.

When you think of the woman you aspire to be, what does she look like, feel like, act like?

How does she spend her time, how does she make money, how does she dress and wear her hair? Visualize and describe her.

What does she see, hear, smell, taste and feel on an average, ideal day?

COMPARISON

Notice a situation where you start comparing yourself to someone else. Write down your thoughts and the feelings they trigger.

What comes to mind when you feel jealous or inadequate?

What irrational fears are you feeding into in those moments?

If you were your own best friend, what would you say to yourself to address those fears and remind you of your value?

In what ways do you feel limited by your uniqueness or empowered by it? How does this affect how you express yourself?

Do you prefer to stand out or go unnoticed? Why or why not?

ACT AS IF

What does confidence feel like? Write the first thing that comes to mind. Then keep going. Keep narrowing it down and getting more specific until you feel satisfied that you are as close to the core feeling as you can get.

Now what activities make you feel this way?

What do you wish you were more confident about? What do you need courage for right now?

What core beliefs can you rely on to give you courage for that situation? Describe the mindset you need to develop to face that situation confidently.

What does wholeness feel like? Write the first thing that comes to mind. Then keep going. Keep narrowing it down and getting more specific until you feel satisfied that you are as close to the core feeling as you can get.

If wholeness could talk, what would it say, specifically to you?

SELF-AFFIRMATION

Make a list of five self-affirming, hope triggering statements you need to hear more often. Put them on sticky notes and place them strategically around your space. If you can commit them to memory, even better. Repeat them when you need strength.

Make a list of five self-doubts or self-critical thoughts that plague you. After each one, replace it with a positive thought that supports the vision you have for yourself. Turn the negatives into positives and repeat those positives every time the old thoughts pop up.

IMPERFECT ACTION

Is there something new that you would like to learn that you've been putting off? If so, why?

Write about a project or endeavor that you started but didn't finish.

What was the motivation behind the project? What was the reason, the "why" of it all, and does that reason still exist?

Why didn't you finish it and what would it take for you to try again?

CONCLUSION

I believe that storytelling heals. I believe in awkward honesty, making mistakes and trusting your journey.

With these beliefs driving me, I developed a plan.

I thought I would take a huge leap of faith that would change my life drastically, then I'd sit back and watch everything fall into place.

Because that is what people say: it all falls into place.

More accurate for me: it all falls apart and you learn to trust the fall.

My plan was to leap, but I didn't think much about what would happen next. I just knew that if I didn't leap, I'd be pushed and I didn't want that to be my story. I was tired of chasing appearances and a lifestyle that my heart didn't want.

So I leaped.

I left my full-time job in finance to build a career out of my writing hobby. This journey is teaching me how important it is to approach both ups and downs with the same willingness. I prayed for a lifestyle change and I got it. But it didn't descend on me out of the sky.

If anything fell, it was me.

I fell out of favor with some, because I decided to focus on myself. I fell off the radar, looking for myself in places where no one could reach me. I fell out of love with old ideas of myself and others that were holding me back. I fell hard for my dreams and my imagination, because I finally started believing that they were mine for a reason.

Along the way I've learned to fall more gracefully. It's not a one-time thing. You fall. You bounce. You soar. It becomes a dance.

Every time you are lifted up and every time you drop, you gain wisdom that expands your mind and opens your heart. How you fall becomes part of your artistry and your growth. If only we could see falling as a sign of progress.

Falling off the pedestal allows you to be free.

Many of us are afraid to fall for ourselves and what we believe in because of what people might say. Because of what is deemed responsible and acceptable and prudent.

I can think of dozens of unsolicited comments I've received from people over the years.

When I got pregnant with three babies without being married. When I went natural. When I quit my job. When I stopped letting people's limitations become my own. When I embraced my style. My pace. My needs. When I dared to be human and emotional and unashamed. Unceasingly, there will be someone who will judge and try to detour you with their disappointment.

The escape from all of that is to let yourself fall. Fall for something that tests your faith and your ability to let go. It's scary to come undone. But it you embrace the fall, you can finesse it and you can make beautiful things along the way.

Thank you for reading this book and thank you for allowing me to support your journey of self-discovery.

EPILOGUE

I promise myself to approach life with an open heart and open mind. Of all the things I value — love, gratitude, authenticity and kindness are foremost.

I choose to focus my efforts on what is important to me, and I release the need to diminish my individuality to avoid judgment.

I embrace my life and my journey as a complex, versatile woman who is full of extreme contrasts, evolving ideas, and a passion for self-discovery.

I commit myself to living Love as a way of life. I commit myself to being authentic in my work and relationships and to accept the truth without fear or resistance.

I will seek to align my values with my message and my actions. I know that this alignment will connect me with my purpose and the community that I intend to serve.

I believe it is my calling to shed light on the generational trauma, mental health issues, and lack of self-love that is so prevalent yet unspoken among women of color in our communities.

I will promote writing as a path to healing and I will stay open to new challenges, address anxiety with action, and never apologize for being who I am.

Before you go, write a promise statement to yourself. When life challenges you, let this statement remind you of who you are.

ABOUT THE AUTHOR

GG Renee Hill is a writer, speaker and advocate for self-discovery through writing.

A candid voice for mental health and self-care, GG writes about the joys and challenges of living an authentic life and becoming a fully expressed woman.

Her books, courses and workshops empower women to embrace all their layers, creatively and shamelessly.

She brings her experience as a blogger, memoirist, ghostwriter and coach to the products and services she offers on her website, allthemanylayers.com.

Currently, she is seeking representation and writing a book of essays about her mental health journey.

GG is on Twitter and Instagram @ggreneewrites.

Made in the USA
Middletown, DE
18 November 2018